OUR AMERICAN GOVERNMENT

What Is It? How Does It Function?

150 QUESTIONS AND ANSWERS

(1977 Edition)

NOVEMBER 3, 1977.—Ordered to be printed

U.S. GOVERNMENT PRINTING OFFICE

98–585 O   WASHINGTON : 1978

H. Con. Res. 205 Passed November 3, 1977

NINETY-FIFTH CONGRESS OF THE UNITED STATES OF AMERICA

AT THE FIRST SESSION

Begun and held at the City of Washington on Tuesday, the fourth day of January, one thousand nine hundred and seventy-seven

CONCURRENT RESOLUTION

Resolved by the House of Representatives (the Senate concurring), That there shall be printed as a House document a revised edition of "Our American Government", revised under the direction of the Joint Committee on Printing.

SEC. 2. In addition to the usual number of copies, there shall be printed five hundred and five thousand additional copies, of which four hundred and forty-three thousand copies shall be for the use of the House of Representatives, fifty-two thousand copies shall be for the use of the Senate, and ten thousand copies shall be for the use of the Joint Committee on Printing.

Attest: EDMUND L. HENSHAW, Jr.,
Clerk of the House of Representatives.

Attest: J. S. KIMMITT,
Secretary of the Senate.

(III)

FOREWORD

This pamphlet provides in question-and-answer form a clear, concise synopsis of our United States Government and our Nation's Capital.

The questions are similar to those often received from constituents by Members of Congress. The information in this booklet includes much that is not readily available elsewhere about the Congress, the Executive and the Judicial branches of Government. It includes a listing of the chairmen of Standing Committees of the House of Representatives and Senate, and Joint and Select Committees, as well as complete state delegations of Representatives and Senators, broken down to Congressional Districts.

It is hoped that the popular, easy-to-follow style of this booklet will encourage many to spend pleasant hours in discussions or quiz-games about our Government and how it works.

FRANK THOMPSON, Jr.,
Chairman, Committee on House Administration.

CONTENTS

STATE DELEGATIONS*
95th Congress
(Jan. 3, 1977–Jan. 3, 1979)

Number which precedes name of Representative designates congressional district. Democrats in roman. Republicans in *italic*. Independent in CAPS

ALABAMA

SENATORS

John J. Sparkman   James B. Allen

REPRESENTATIVES

[Democrats, 4; Republicans, 3]

1. *Jack Edwards*
2. *William L. Dickinson*
3. Bill Nichols
4. Tom Bevill
5. Ronnie G. Flippo
6. *John Buchanan*
7. Walter Flowers

ALASKA

SENATORS

Ted Stevens   Mike Gravel

REPRESENTATIVE

[Republican, 1]

At large—*Donald E. Young*

ARIZONA

SENATORS

Barry Goldwater   Dennis DeConcini

REPRESENTATIVES

[Democrats, 2; Republicans, 2]

1. *John J. Rhodes*
2. Morris K. Udall
3. Bob Stump
4. *Eldon D. Rudd*

ARKANSAS

SENATORS

Dale Bumpers   Kaneaster Hodges, Jr.

REPRESENTATIVES

[Democrats, 3; Republican, 1]

1. Bill Alexander
2. James G. Tucker, Jr.
3. *John P. Hammerschmidt*
4. Ray Thornton

CALIFORNIA

SENATORS

Alan Cranston   *S. I. Hayakawa*

REPRESENTATIVES

[Democrats, 29; Republicans, 14]

1. Harold T. Johnson
2. *Don H. Clausen*
3. John E. Moss
4. Robert L. Leggett
5. John Burton
6. Phillip Burton
7. George Miller
8. Ronald V. Dellums
9. Fortney H. (Pete) Stark
10. Don Edwards
11. Leo J. Ryan
12. *Paul N. (Pete) McCloskey, Jr.*
13. Norman Y. Mineta
14. John J. McFall
15. B. F. Sisk
16. Leon E. Panetta
17. John Krebs
18. *William M. Ketchum*
19. *Robert J. Lagomarsino*
20. *Barry Goldwater, Jr.*
21. James C. Corman
22. *Carlos J. Moorhead*
23. Anthony C. Beilenson
24. Henry A. Waxman
25. Edward R. Roybal
26. *John Rousselot*
27. *Robert K. Dornan*
28. Yvonne Brathwaite Burke
29. Augustus F. (Gus) Hawkins
30. George E. Danielson
31. Charles H. Wilson
32. Glenn M. Anderson
33. *Del Clawson*
34. Mark W. Hannaford
35. Jim Lloyd
36. George E. Brown, Jr.
37. *Shirley N. Pettis*
38. Jerry M. Patterson
39. *Charles E. Wiggins*
40. *Robert E. Badham*
41. *Bob Wilson*
42. Lionel Van Deerlin
43. *Clair W. Burgener*

*Listing is updated to Feb. 22, 1978.

(IX)

COLORADO

SENATORS

Floyd K. Haskell   Gary Hart

REPRESENTATIVES

[Democrats, 3; Republicans, 2]

1. Patricia Schroeder
2. Timothy E. Wirth
3. Frank E. Evans
4. *James P. (Jim) Johnson*
5. *William L. Armstrong*

CONNECTICUT

SENATORS

Abraham A. Ribicoff   *Lowell P. Weicker, Jr.*

REPRESENTATIVES

[Democrats, 4; Republicans, 2]

1. William R. Cotter
2. Christopher J. Dodd
3. Robert N. Giaimo
4. *Stewart B. McKinney*
5. *Ronald A. Sarasin*
6. Toby Moffett

DELAWARE

SENATORS

William V. Roth, Jr.   Joseph R. Biden, Jr.

REPRESENTATIVE

[Republican, 1]

At large—*Thomas B. Evans, Jr.*

FLORIDA

SENATORS

Lawton Chiles   Richard (Dick) Stone

REPRESENTATIVES

[Democrats, 10; Republicans, 5]

1. Robert L. F. Sikes
2. Don Fuqua
3. Charles E. Bennett
4. Bill Chappell, Jr.
5. *Richard Kelly*
6. *C. W. Bill Young*
7. Sam M. Gibbons
8. Andrew P. Ireland
9. *Louis Frey, Jr.*
10. *L. A. (Skip) Bafalis*
11. Paul G. Rogers
12. *J. Herbert Burke*
13. William Lehman
14. Claude D. Pepper
15. Dante B. Fascell

GEORGIA

SENATORS

Herman E. Talmadge   Sam Nunn

REPRESENTATIVES

[Democrats, 10]

1. Bo Ginn
2. Dawson Mathis
3. Jack Brinkley
4. Elliott H. Levitas
5. Wyche Fowler, Jr.
6. John J. Flynt, Jr.
7. Larry McDonald
8. Billy Lee Evans
9. Edgar L. Jenkins
10. D. Douglas Barnard, Jr.

HAWAII

SENATORS

Daniel K. Inouye   Spark M. Matsunaga

REPRESENTATIVES
[Democrats, 2]

1. Cecil Heftel   2. Daniel K. Akaka

IDAHO

SENATORS

Frank Church   *James A. McClure*

REPRESENTATIVES
[Republicans, 2]

1. *Steven D. Symms*   2. *George Hansen*

ILLINOIS

SENATORS

Charles H. Percy   Adlai E. Stevenson

REPRESENTATIVES
[Democrats, 12; Republicans, 12]

1. Ralph H. Metcalfe
2. Morgan F. Murphy
3. Martin A. Russo
4. *Edward J. Derwinski*
5. John G. Fary
6. *Henry J. Hyde*
7. Cardiss Collins
8. Dan Rostenkowski
9. Sidney R. Yates
10. Abner J. Mikva
11. Frank Annunzio
12. *Philip M. Crane*
13. *Robert McClory*
14. *John N. Erlenborn*
15. *Thomas J. Corcoran*
16. *John B. Anderson*
17. *George M. O'Brien*
18. *Robert H. Michel*
19. *Thomas F. Railsback*
20. *Paul Findley*
21. *Edward R. Madigan*
22. George E. Shipley
23. Melvin Price
24. Paul Simon

INDIANA

SENATORS

Birch Bayh   *Richard G. Lugar*

REPRESENTATIVES
[Democrats, 8; Republicans, 3]

1. Adam Benjamin, Jr.
2. Floyd J. Fithian
3. John Brademas
4. *J. Danforth Quayle*
5. *Elwood Hillis*
6. David W. Evans
7. *John T. Myers*
8. David L. Cornwell
9. Lee H. Hamilton
10. Philip R. Sharp
11. Andrew Jacobs, Jr.

IOWA

SENATORS

Dick Clark   John C. Culver

REPRESENTATIVES
[Democrats, 4; Republicans, 2]

1. *James A. S. Leach*
2. Michael T. Blouin
3. *Charles E. Grassley*
4. Neal Smith
5. Tom Harkin
6. Berkley Bedell

KANSAS

SENATORS

James B. Pearson   *Bob Dole*

REPRESENTATIVES

[Democrats, 2; Republicans, 3]

1. *Keith G. Sebelius*   3. *Larry Winn, Jr.*   5. *Joe Skubitz*
2. Martha Keys   4. Daniel R. Glickman

KENTUCKY

SENATORS

Walter (Dee) Huddleston   Wendell H. Ford

REPRESENTATIVES

[Democrats, 5; Republicans, 2]

1. Carroll Hubbard, Jr.   4. *M. G. (Gene) Snyder*   6. John Breckinridge
2. William H. Natcher   5. *Tim Lee Carter*   7. Carl D. Perkins
3. Romano L. Mazzoli

LOUISIANA

SENATORS

Russell B. Long   J. Bennett Johnston, Jr.

REPRESENTATIVES

[Democrats, 5; Republicans, 3]

1. *Robert L. Livingston*   3. *David C. Treen*   6. *W. Henson Moore*
2. Corrine C. (Lindy)   4. Joe D. Waggonner, Jr.   7. John B. Breaux
   Boggs   5. Thomas J. Huckaby   8. Gillis W. Long

MAINE

SENATORS

Edmund S. Muskie   William D. Hathaway

REPRESENTATIVES

[Republicans, 2]

1. *David F. Emery*   2. *William S. Cohen*

MARYLAND

SENATORS

Charles McC. Mathias, Jr.   Paul S. Sarbanes

REPRESENTATIVES

[Democrats, 5; Republicans, 3]

1. *Robert E. Bauman*   4. *Marjorie S. Holt*   7. Parren J. Mitchell
2. Clarence D. Long   5. Gladys Noon Spellman   8. *Newton I. Steers, Jr.*
3. Barbara A. Mikulski   6. Goodloe E. Byron

MASSACHUSETTS

SENATORS

Edward M. Kennedy   *Edward W. Brooke*

REPRESENTATIVES

[Democrats, 10; Republicans, 2]

1. *Silvio O. Conte*
2. Edward P. Boland
3. Joseph D. Early
4. Robert F. Drinan
5. Paul E. Tsongas
6. Michael J. Harrington
7. Edward J. Markey
8. Thomas P. O'Neill, Jr.
9. John Joseph Moakley
10. *Margaret M. Heckler*
11. James A. Burke
12. Gerry E. Studds

MICHIGAN

SENATORS

Robert P. Griffin   Donald W. Riegle, Jr.

REPRESENTATIVES

[Democrats, 11; Republicans, 8]

1. John Conyers, Jr.
2. *Carl D. Pursell*
3. *Garry E. Brown*
4. *David A. Stockman*
5. *Harold S. Sawyer*
6. Bob Carr
7. Dale E. Kildee
8. Bob Traxler
9. *Guy Vander Jagt*
10. *Elford A. Cederberg*
11. *Philip E. Ruppe*
12. David E. Bonior
13. Charles C. Diggs, Jr.
14. Lucien N. Nedzi
15. William D. Ford
16. John D. Dingell
17. William M. Brodhead
18. James J. Blanchard
19. *William S. Broomfield*

MINNESOTA

SENATORS

Wendell R. Anderson   Muriel Humphrey

REPRESENTATIVES

[Democrats, 4; Republicans, 4]

1. *Albert H. Quie*
2. *Tom Hagedorn*
3. *Bill Frenzel*
4. Bruce F. Vento
5. Donald M. Fraser
6. Richard Nolan
7. *Arlan Stangeland*
8. James L. Oberstar

MISSISSIPPI

SENATORS

James O. Eastland   John C. Stennis

REPRESENTATIVES

[Democrats, 3; Republicans, 2]

1. Jamie L. Whitten
2. David R. Bowen
3. G. V. (Sonny) Montgomery
4. *Thad Cochran*
5. *Trent Lott*

MISSOURI

SENATORS

Thomas F. Eagleton   *John C. Danforth*

REPRESENTATIVES

[Democrats, 8; Republicans, 2]

1. William (Bill) Clay
2. Robert A. Young
3. Richard A. Gephardt
4. Ike Skelton
5. Richard Bolling
6. *E. Thomas Coleman*
7. *Gene Taylor*
8. Richard H. Ichord
9. Harold L. Volkmer
10. Bill D. Burlison

MONTANA

SENATORS

John Melcher   Paul G. Hatfield

REPRESENTATIVES

[Democrat, 1; Republican, 1]

1. Max Baucus   2. *Ron Marlenee*

NEBRASKA

SENATORS

Carl T. Curtis   Edward Zorinsky

REPRESENTATIVES

[Democrat, 1; Republicans, 2]

1. *Charles Thone*   2. John J. Cavanaugh   3. *Virginia Smith*

NEVADA

SENATORS

Howard W. Cannon   *Paul Laxalt*

REPRESENTATIVE

[Democrat, 1]

At large—Jim Santini

NEW HAMPSHIRE

SENATORS

Thomas J. McIntyre   John A. Durkin

REPRESENTATIVES

[Democrat, 1; Republican, 1]

1. Norman E. D'Amours   2. *James C. Cleveland*

NEW JERSEY

SENATORS

Clifford P. Case   Harrison A. Williams, Jr.

REPRESENTATIVES
[Democrats, 11; Republicans, 4]

1. James J. Florio
2. William J. Hughes
3. James J. Howard
4. Frank Thompson, Jr.
5. *Millicent Fenwick*
6. *Edwin B. Forsythe*
7. Andrew Maguire
8. Robert A. Roe
9. *Harold C. Hollenbeck*
10. Peter W. Rodino, Jr.
11. Joseph G. Minish
12. *Matthew J. Rinaldo*
13. Helen S. Meyner
14. Joseph A. LeFante
15. Edward J. Patten

NEW MEXICO

SENATORS

Pete V. Domenici   *Harrison H. Schmitt*

REPRESENTATIVES
[Democrat, 1; Republican, 1]

1. *Manuel Lujan, Jr.*   2. Harold Runnels

NEW YORK

SENATORS

Jacob K. Javits   Daniel P. Moynihan

REPRESENTATIVES
[Democrats, 27; Republicans, 12]

1. Otis G. Pike
2. Thomas J. Downey
3. Jerome A. Ambro
4. *Norman F. Lent*
5. *John W. Wydler*
6. Lester L. Wolff
7. Joseph P. Addabbo
8. Benjamin S. Rosenthal
9. James J. Delaney
10. Mario Biaggi
11. James H. Scheuer
12. Shirley Chisholm
13. Stephen J. Solarz
14. Frederick W. Richmond
15. Leo C. Zeferetti
16. Elizabeth Holtzman
17. John M. Murphy
18. *S. William Green*
19. Charles B. Rangel
20. Ted Weiss
21. Robert Garcia
22. Jonathan B. Bingham
23. *Bruce F. Caputo*
24. Richard L. Ottinger
25. *Hamilton Fish, Jr.*
26. *Benjamin A. Gilman*
27. Matthew F. McHugh
28. Samuel S. Stratton
29. Edward W. Pattison
30. *Robert C. McEwen*
31. *Donald J. Mitchell*
32. James M. Hanley
33. *William F. Walsh*
34. *Frank Horton*
35. *Barber B. Conable, Jr.*
36. John J. LaFalce
37. Henry J. Nowak
38. *Jack Kemp*
39. Stanley N. Lundine

NORTH CAROLINA

SENATORS

Jesse A. Helms   Robert Morgan

REPRESENTATIVES
[Democrats, 9; Republicans, 2]

1. Walter B. Jones
2. L. H. Fountain
3. Charles O. Whitley, Sr.
4. Ike F. Andrews
5. Stephen L. Neal
6. Richardson Preyer
7. Charles Rose
8. W. G. (Bill) Hefner
9. *James G. Martin*
10. *James T. Broyhill*
11. V. Lamar Gudger

NORTH DAKOTA

SENATORS

Milton R. Young   Quentin N. Burdick

REPRESENTATIVE

[Republican, 1]

At large—*Mark Andrews*

OHIO

SENATORS

John Glenn   Howard M. Metzenbaum

REPRESENTATIVES

[Democrats, 10; Republicans, 13]

1. *Willis D. Gradison, Jr.*	9. Thomas L. Ashley	17. *John M. Ashbrook*
2. Thomas A. Luken	10. *Clarence E. Miller*	18. Douglas Applegate
3. *Charles W. Whalen, Jr.*	11. *J. William Stanton*	19. Charles J. Carney
4. *Tennyson Guyer*	12. *Samuel L. Devine*	20. Mary Rose Oakar
5. *Delbert L. Latta*	13. Donald J. Pease	21. Louis Stokes
6. *William H. Harsha*	14. John F. Seiberling	22. Charles A. Vanik
7. *Clarence J. Brown*	15. *Chalmers P. Wylie*	23. Ronald M. Mottl
8. *Thomas N. Kindness*	16. *Ralph S. Regula*	

OKLAHOMA

SENATORS

Henry L. Bellmon   *Dewey F. Bartlett*

REPRESENTATIVES

[Democrats, 5; Republican, 1]

1. James R. Jones	3. Wesley W. Watkins	5. *Mickey Edwards*
2. Ted Risenhoover	4. Tom Steed	6. Glenn English

OREGON

SENATORS

Mark O. Hatfield   *Bob Packwood*

REPRESENTATIVES

[Democrats, 4]

1. Les AuCoin	3. Robert Duncan	4. James Weaver
2. Al Ullman		

PENNSYLVANIA

SENATORS

Richard S. Schweiker   *H. John Heinz 3d*

REPRESENTATIVES

[Democrats, 17; Republicans, 8]

1. Michael O. Myers
2. Robert N. C. Nix
3. Raymond F. Lederer
4. Joshua Eilberg
5. *Richard T. Schulze*
6. Gus Yatron
7. Robert W. Edgar
8. Peter H. Kostmayer
9. *E. G. (Bud) Shuster*
10. *Joseph M. McDade*
11. Daniel J. Flood
12. John P. Murtha
13. *Lawrence Coughlin*
14. William S. Moorhead
15. Fred B. Rooney
16. *Robert S. Walker*
17. Allen E. Ertel
18. Doug Walgren
19. *William F. Goodling*
20. Joseph M. Gaydos
21. John H. Dent
22. Austin J. Murphy
23. Joseph S. Ammerman
24. *Marc L. Marks*
25. *Gary A. Myers*

RHODE ISLAND

SENATORS

Claiborne Pell   *John H. Chafee*

REPRESENTATIVES

[Democrats, 2]

1. Fernand J. St Germain   2. Edward P. Beard

SOUTH CAROLINA

SENATORS

Strom Thurmond   Ernest F. Hollings

REPRESENTATIVES

[Democrats, 5; Republican, 1]

1. Mendel J. Davis
2. *Floyd Spence*
3. Butler Derrick
4. James R. Mann
5. Kenneth L. Holland
6. John W. Jenrette, Jr.

SOUTH DAKOTA

SENATORS

George McGovern   James Abourezk

REPRESENTATIVES

[Republicans, 2]

1. *Larry Pressler*   2. *James Abdnor*

TENNESSEE

SENATORS

Howard H. Baker, Jr.   James R. Sasser

REPRESENTATIVES

[Democrats, 5; Republicans, 3]

1. *James H. Quillen*
2. *John J. Duncan*
3. Marilyn Lloyd
4. Albert A. Gore, Jr.
5. Clifford R. Allen
6. *Robin L. Beard*
7. Ed Jones
8. Harold E. Ford

TEXAS

SENATORS

John G. Tower   Lloyd M. Bentsen

REPRESENTATIVES

[Democrats, 22; Republicans, 2]

1. Sam B. Hall, Jr.
2. Charles Wilson
3. *James M. Collins*
4. Ray Roberts
5. James A. Mattox
6. Olin E. Teague
7. *Bill Archer*
8. Bob Eckhardt
9. Jack Brooks
10. J. J. (Jake) Pickle
11. W. R. Poage
12. James C. Wright, Jr.
13. Jack Hightower
14. John Young
15. E (Kika) de la Garza
16. Richard C. White
17. Omar Burleson
18. Barbara Jordan
19. George H. Mahon
20. Henry B. Gonzalez
21. Robert (Bob) Krueger
22. Robert A. Gammage
23. Abraham Kazen, Jr.
24. Dale Milford

UTAH

SENATORS

Jake Garn   *Orrin G. Hatch*

REPRESENTATIVES

[Democrat, 1; Republican, 1]

1. K. Gunn McKay   2. *David D. Marriott*

VERMONT

SENATORS

Robert T. Stafford   Patrick J. Leahy

REPRESENTATIVE

[Republican, 1]

At large—James M. Jeffords

VIRGINIA

SENATORS

HARRY F. BYRD, JR.   *William Lloyd Scott*

REPRESENTATIVES

[Democrats, 4; Republicans, 6]

1. *Paul S. Trible, Jr.*
2. *G. William Whitehurst*
3. David E. Satterfield 3d
4. *Robert W. Daniel, Jr.*
5. W. C. (Dan) Daniel
6. *M. Caldwell Butler*
7. *J. Kenneth Robinson*
8. Herbert E. Harris 2d
9. *William C. Wampler*
10. Joseph L. Fisher

WASHINGTON

SENATORS

Warren G. Magnuson   Henry M. Jackson

REPRESENTATIVES

[Democrats, 5; Republicans, 2]

1. *Joel Pritchard*
2. Lloyd Meeds
3. Don Bonker
4. Mike McCormack
5. Thomas S. Foley
6. Norman D. Dicks
7. *John E. Cunningham*

WEST VIRGINIA

SENATORS

Jennings Randolph   Robert C. Byrd

REPRESENTATIVES
[Democrats, 4]

1. Robert H. Mollohan   3. John Slack   4. Nick J. Rahall 2d
2. Harley O. Staggers

WISCONSIN

SENATORS

William Proxmire   Gaylord Nelson

REPRESENTATIVES

[Democrats, 7; Republicans, 2]

1. Les Aspin   4. Clement J. Zablocki   7. David R. Obey
2. Robert W. Kastenmeier   5. Henry S. Reuss   8. Robert J. Cornell
3. Alvin Baldus   6. *William A. Steiger*   9. *Robert W. Kasten, Jr.*

WYOMING

SENATORS

Clifford P. Hansen   *Malcolm Wallop*

REPRESENTATIVES
[Democrat, 1]

At large—Teno Roncalio

DISTRICT OF COLUMBIA

DELEGATE
[Democrat, 1]

Walter E. Fauntroy

GUAM

DELEGATE
[Democrat, 1]

Antonio Borja Won Pat

PUERTO RICO

RESIDENT COMMISSIONER
[New Progressive, 1]

Baltasar Corrada

VIRGIN ISLANDS

DELEGATE
[Democrat, 1]

Ron de Lugo

CLASSIFICATION*

SENATE		HOUSE	
Democrats	61	Democrats	292
Republicans	38	Republicans	143
Independent	1		
		Total	435
Total	100		

*Totals at beginning of 95th Cong., Jan. 3, 1977.

OUR AMERICAN GOVERNMENT

DEMOCRACY AND ITS AMERICAN SOURCES

1. What is the purpose of the American Government?

The purpose is expressed in the preamble to the Constitution: "We the People of the United States, in Order to form a more perfect Union, establish Justice, insure domestic Tranquility, provide for the common defence, promote the general Welfare, and secure the Blessings of Liberty to ourselves and our Posterity, do ordain and establish this Constitution for the United States of America."

2. What form of government do we have in the United States?

With the exception of town meetings, a form of pure democracy, we have at the local, state, and national levels a democratic, representative, republican form of government. It is "democratic" because the people govern themselves; "representative" because they do so through elected representatives chosen by ballot; and "republican" because the government derives its powers from the people.

3. What were the Articles of Confederation?

The Articles of Confederation were a framework of national government which the Continental Congress agreed upon on Nov. 17, 1777. This was proposed to the legislatures of all the states with a circular letter, recommending the Articles as containing the only plan of union which stood a chance of being adopted by the separate states. Thus, if the states approved, they could authorize their delegates in Congress to ratify the Articles.

By March 1, 1781, the Articles had been ratified by all thirteen states and on the following day Congress assembled under the new form of government.

4. What contributions has our country made to the institution of government?

Some of the American contributions to the institution of government are as follows: a written constitution, an independent judiciary to interpret it, and division of powers between the Federal and state governments.

5. What were the six basic principles on which the Constitution was framed?

The Fathers of the Constitution agreed, without dispute, to six basic principles:

1. It was understood that all states would be equal. The national Government cannot give special privileges to one state.

2. There should be three branches of government—one to make the laws, another to execute them, and a third to settle questions of law.

1

3. All persons are equal before the law; and anyone, rich or poor, can demand the protection of the law in the exercise of his rights.

4. The Government is a government of laws, not of men. No one is above the law. No officer of the Government can use authority unless the Constitution or the law permits.

· 5. The people can change the authority of the Government by changing the Constitution. (One such change was the election of Senators by direct vote instead of by state legislatures.)

6. The Constitution, the Acts of Congress, and the treaties of the U.S. are law, the highest in the land. The national Government is a government of the people, and not of the states alone.

THE CONSTITUTION

6. What is the "supreme law of the land"?

The Constitution, laws of the United States made "in pursuance of" the Constitution, and treaties made under authority of the United States. Judges throughout the country are bound by them, regardless of anything in separate State constitutions or laws.

7. What is meant by the "separation of powers" in the Federal Government?

The Constitution contains provisions in separate articles for three great departments of government—legislative, executive, and judicial. There is a significant difference in the grants of power to these departments: The first article, treating of legislative power, vests in Congress "all legislative Powers herein granted"; the second article vests "the executive Power" in the President; and the third article states that "The judicial Power of the United States shall be vested in one Supreme Court and in such inferior courts as the Congress may from time to time ordain and establish." The theory of this separation of powers is that by keeping them independent of each other they are a check upon each other so that a tyrannous concentration of unchecked power is made impossible.

8. What is the Bill of Rights?

The first 10 amendments to the Constitution, adopted in 1791, are commonly referred to as the Bill of Rights. As a matter of fact, the first 8 really set out the substantive and procedural personal rights associated with that description, while 9 and 10 are general rules of interpretation of the relation between the State and Federal governments—all powers not delegated by the Constitution to the United States, nor prohibited to the States, being reserved to the States or the people.

9. What are the rights enumerated in the Bill of Rights?

It should be noted that the Bill of Rights is in form primarily a bill of "don'ts" for Congress—in other words, it is not a theoretical enumeration, but a series of prohibitions on the enactment by Congress of laws infringing certain rights. Aside from the three perhaps most commonly discussed—freedom of religion, speech, and press—the rights include:

Right to assemble, and to petition Congress (amendment 1)
Right to bear arms (amendment 2)

Right not to have soldiers quartered in one's home in peacetime, except as prescribed by law (amendment 3)

Right to be secure against "unreasonable searches and seizures" (amendment 4)

Right in general not to be held to answer criminal charges except upon indictment (amendment 5)

Right not to be put twice in jeopardy for the same offense (amendment 5)

Right not to be compelled to be a witness against oneself (amendment 5)

Right not to be deprived of life, liberty, or property without due process of law (amendment 5)

Right to just compensation for private property, taken for public use (amendment 5)

Right, in criminal prosecution, to trial by a jury—to be notified of the charges, to be confronted with witnesses, to have compulsory process for calling witnesses, and to have legal counsel (amendment 6)

Right to a jury trial in suits at law involving over twenty dollars (amendment 7)

Right not to have excessive bail required, nor excessive fines imposed, nor cruel and unusual punishments inflicted (amendment 8)

10. How may the Constitution be amended?

Amendments may be proposed on the initiative of Congress (by two-thirds vote in each House) or by convention (on application of two-thirds of the State legislatures). So far, there has never been a convention called under this authority. Ratification may, at the discretion of Congress, be either by the legislatures or by conventions, in three-fourths of the States. As of the adjournment of the 94th Congress, the 21st amendment is the only one to have been ratified by State conventions.

The first 10 amendments were practically a part of the original instrument (being ratified in 1791), the 11th amendment was ratified in 1795, and the 12th amendment in 1804. Thereafter, no amendment was added to the Constitution for 60 years. After the Civil War, three amendments were ratified (1865–70), followed by another long interval before the 16th amendment became effective in 1913.

The most recent amendment, the 26th, was ratified on July 1, 1971. It lowered the voting age to 18 for Federal, State, and local elections. At present one amendment is pending before the States, to provide equal rights for men and women. As of December 1977, thirty-five of the required thirty-eight States had ratified it. Of these, however, Nebraska, Tennessee, and Idaho have rescinded their ratifications. Whether Congress would accept such rescissions is, however, doubtful.

11. Have many amendments to the Constitution been repealed?

Only one—the 18th amendment (prohibition), which was repealed by the 21st amendment.

12. How long may a proposed amendment remain outstanding and open to ratification?

The Supreme Court has stated that ratification must be within "some reasonable time after the proposal." Beginning with the 18th amendment it has been customary for Congress to set a definite period for ratification. In the case of the 18th, 20th, 21st, and 22d amendments, and the pending equal rights amendment, the period set was 7 years; but there has been no determination as to just how long a "reasonable time" might extend.

13. What is the "lame duck" amendment?

The 20th amendment to the Constitution, proclaimed by the Secretary of State on February 6, 1933, to have been ratified by sufficient States to make it a part of the Constitution. This amendment provides, among other things, that the terms of the President and Vice President shall end at noon on January 20; the terms of Senators and Representatives shall end at noon on January 3 instead of March 4, and the terms of their successors shall then begin. Prior to this amendment, the annual session of Congress began on the first Monday in December (Constitution, art. I, sec. 4). Since the terms of new members formerly began on March 4, this meant that members who had been defeated or did not stand for reelection in November continued to serve during the "lame duck" session from December through March 4. Adoption of the 20th amendment has not entirely obviated legislation by a Congress that does not represent the latest choice of the people. Eight sessions since 1933 have not adjourned *sine die* prior to the November general elections. The most recent Congress to extend beyond the November elections was the 93d Congress which adjourned on December 20, 1974.

THE ELECTORAL PROCESS

14. What is the electoral college?

The Constitution provides that each State "shall appoint * * * a number of electors" equal to the combined number of its Senators and Representatives and, in the 23d amendment, that the District of Columbia shall have as many electors as the least populous State (at present 3). In the 1972 presidential election, accordingly, 538 electors cast ballots for President and Vice President, with 270 necessary for election.

The framers of the Constitution thought that a convention of qualified electors would be the best way to choose a President. They contemplated that electors would not be pledged to any particular candidate but would calmly and wisely decide who should be President. The rapid development of political parties, however, nullified this notion and for many years the electoral college has simply ratified the choice of the voters in each State, although occasionally an elector will "bolt" and "vote his conscience."

The electors whose party wins in a State's balloting for President meet at a place designated by the State legislature, usually the State capital. They meet on the Monday following the second Wednesday in December in a presidential election year and vote as a unit for their candidate. Six copies of these votes are made. One is for the President of the United States Senate; 2 for the secretary of state; 2 for the Secretary of State of the United States; and 1 for the district judge. The count of all electoral ballots takes place in joint session of Congress every 4 years on January 6.

15. Did the electoral college ever vote unanimously for any President other than George Washington?

No. In the election of Monroe in 1820, one elector, William Plumer, voted against Monroe. Contrary to popular myth Plumer voted against James Monroe because he considered him a weak President, and not because he wanted Washington to be the only President to receive the electoral college's unanimous vote.

16. Why is election day on the Tuesday after the first Monday in November?

Despite a constitutional provision that "Congress may determine the time of choosing the electors, and the day on which they shall give their votes; which day shall be the same throughout the United States," no national day of election was set until 1845, though Congress had provided in 1792 for the first Wednesday in December as the day for presidential electors to meet and cast their votes, and further had provided in that law for electors to be chosen within 34 days of the date on which they were to meet.

The impetus for setting a national election day was popular election of presidential electors and fraud attendant therewith because of different dates for election in the several States. Wagonloads of persons would be transported across State boundaries in order to cast ballots in other than their home State. The incidence of election fraud was widespread enough to arouse agitation for a national election day. Consequently, Congress enacted one in 1845. The Tuesday after the first Monday in November was chosen because it fell approximately 30 days prior to the date on which electors were to assemble to cast their ballots for President and Vice President. Tuesday was chosen to permit persons who had to travel some distance to the polls to do so on Monday rather than Sunday, a day of worship for Christians. The Tuesday after the first Monday also was chosen to guarantee against election day falling on the first day of the month, which would have been a bad day for business.

Over the years, the States have come to adopt this same day as the date for their general elections. This is not true for all State and local elections, however.

In recent years there has been discussion in Congress to change election day to Saturday or Sunday in order to encourage a higher turnout of voters. The arguments which favored the date chosen in 1845, it is now contended, no longer are persuasive.

17. Who is responsible for the regulation of elections in the U.S.?

The regulation of elections is the responsibility of the States subject to the requirements of the Federal Constitution. The Constitution provides, and the Supreme Court has ruled, that Congress has the power to regulate Federal elections in order to maintain the purity of the electoral process, and State elections in order that they be in conformance with constitutional requirements.

For most of our history congressional regulation was minimal. In recent years, however, Congress has enacted considerable legislation to regulate elections. In addition, five amendments to the Constitution directly bear on the regulation of elections (the 14th, 15th, 19th, 24th, and 26th). Since 1957, Congress, exercising its constitutional authority, has enacted laws designed to prevent racial discrimination in the electoral process (the Civil Rights Acts of 1957, 1960, and 1964). In 1965, Congress enacted a Voting Rights Act which effectively eliminated for a stated period of time all tests and similar devices which it found had been used to discriminate against minority groups, particularly black Americans. The same legislation authorized Federal officers to register voters and to observe elections in order to insure that there was no discrimination. In 1970, Congress extended for an additional period of time the test suspension features of the 1965 act; additionally removed unreasonable residence requirements as they applied to voting for President and Vice President; and enfranchised all citizens between 18 and 21. A short time later the Supreme Court held that Congress could lower the voting age only for Federal elections. This curtailment paved the way for rapid adoption of the 26th amendment.

18. What Federal laws regulate political campaign financing?

Until 1972, the Corrupt Practices Acts regulated spending in Federal elections, but only for general and special elections. With passage of the Federal Election Campaign Act of 1971 and subsequent amendments passed in 1974 and 1976, there is now much greater regulation of the Federal elective process—primary, general, and special elections, caucuses, and conventions. The 1971, 1974, and 1976 Acts established strict reporting regulations for all candidates for Federal office and for campaign committees. Contributions are limited. Furthermore, full, though optional, public financing is provided for major party Presidential candidates in the general election and major party national nominating conventions, and matching public funding is provided in Presidential primary elections. Partial funding is provided for other Presidential candidates in the general election. Expenditures by candidates accepting public funds are limited, as are the personal funds such a candidate may spend on his or her own campaign. An independent Federal Elections Commission is the principal enforcement agency given primary civil jurisdiction and investigatory authority in criminal cases. It also has the power to prescribe rules to implement and clarify campaign regulations.

The income tax laws permit political contributions to be deducted or credited against tax owed to the Federal government. Taxpayers who itemize are allowed to deduct up to $200 on a joint return; $100 on a single return. Alternatively, a taxpayer may credit, against his tax owed, up to a maximum of $50 on a joint return and $25 on any other return.

THE CONGRESS

General

19. What is the Congress?

The Congress of the United States is the legislative department of the National Government, and consists of two branches—the Senate and the House of Representatives.

20. What are the powers of Congress as provided in the Constitution?

The Constitution (Article I, Section 8) empowers the Congress to levy taxes, collect revenue, borrow money, regulate interstate and foreign commerce, establish uniform rules of naturalization and bankruptcy, coin money and fix its value, punish counterfeiters, establish a postal system, enact patent and copyright laws, establish Federal courts inferior to the Supreme Court, declare war and provide for armed forces, spend and tax for the "general welfare," and to have exclusive legislative power over the District of Columbia. Congress is also given the power to enact such laws as may be "necessary and proper" to implement its mandate in Article I, and in certain Amendments to the Constitution.

21. What is the term of a Congress, and how often must it meet?

A Congress begins at noon January 3 of each odd-numbered year, and continues for two years, regardless of the number of regular or special sessions held. A session of Congress usually means that both the Senate and House are meeting for the transaction of business.

The Legislative Reorganization Act of 1970 requires Congress to adjourn *sine die* not later than July 31 of each year unless there is a declared war, or unless Congress otherwise provides. In odd numbered years, the Congress must take an August recess if it fails to adjourn by July 31.

22. What is a Congressman?

A Congressman is a Member of either the Senate or the House of Representatives. However, a Member of the Senate is usually referred to as a Senator and a Member of the House as a Congressman. The official title of a Member of the House is "Representative in Congress."

23. What is a Delegate or Resident Commissioner, as distinguished from a Congressman?

The office of Delegate was established by ordinance of the Continental Congress and confirmed by a law of Congress. From the beginning of the Republic, accordingly, the House has admitted Delegates from territories or districts organized by law. Delegates, or Resident Commissioners, may participate in House debate but they are not permitted to vote on the floor. Presently there are a Resident Commissioner and three Delegates in the House (the Resident Commissioner from Puerto Rico, since July 1946; Delegate from the District of Columbia, since March 1971; and Delegates from the Virgin Islands and Guam since January 1973). All serve on committees of the House and possess powers and privileges equivalent to other members of committees.

24. What are the salaries and allowances of Congressmen, Delegates, and Resident Commissioners?

Each Member of Congress (including Delegates and Commissioners) receives a salary of $57,500 per annum. The President *pro tempore* of the Senate and the Majority and Minority Leaders of the House and Senate, and the Deputy President *pro tempore* of the Senate (if any), each receives $65,000 per annum. The Speaker of the House receives $75,000, as does the President *pro tempore* when there is no Vice-President. Members also receive allowances for clerical staff, office equipment rental in Washington and in their home states or districts, home state office space rentals, stationery, postage (air mail and special delivery allowances, in addition to authorized use of the congressional frank), telephone and telegraph expenses, travel, and official office expenses. Members with five years service become eligible for a pension if they participate in the Federal retirement system.

25. How many Members does each State have in the Senate and House of Representatives?

Each State, by the Constitution, is always entitled to two Senators and at least one Representative. Additional House seats are apportioned on the basis of population. Under the apportionment based on the 1970 census—effective commencing with the 93d Congress which convened in January of 1973—the 50 States have the following number of Representatives (apportionments for the 92d Congress, based on the 1960 census, are also shown—in parentheses—for States which gained or lost House seats because of population shifts): Alabama, 7 (8); Alaska, 1; Arizona, 4 (3); Arkansas, 4; California, 43 (38); Colorado, 5 (4); Connecticut, 6; Delaware, 1; Florida, 15 (12); Georgia, 10; Hawaii, 2; Idaho, 2; Illinois, 24; Indiana, 11; Iowa, 6 (7); Kansas, 5; Kentucky, 7; Louisiana, 8; Maine, 2; Maryland, 8; Massachusetts, 12; Michigan, 19; Minnesota, 8; Mississippi, 5; Missouri, 10; Montana, 2; Nebraska, 3; Nevada, 1; New Hampshire, 2; New Jersey, 15; New Mexico, 2; New York, 39 (41); North Carolina, 11; North Dakota, 1 (2); Ohio, 23 (24); Oklahoma, 6; Oregon, 4; Pennsylvania, 25 (27); Rhode Island, 2; South Carolina, 6; South Dakota, 2; Tennessee, 8 (9); Texas, 24 (23); Utah, 2; Vermont, 1; Virginia, 10; Washington, 7; West Virginia, 4 (5); Wisconsin, 9 (10); and Wyoming, 1.

26. In correspondence, how should one address a Member?

When writing to a Member, the form of address is as follows: Hon. John Jones, M.C., House (or Senate) Office Building, Washington, D.C. The ZIP code for the House is 20515; the Senate is 20510. A woman Member of the House is referred to as "the Congresswoman from ———", in correspondence, she should be addressed as "Dear Representative." In the Senate, Members are referred to as "the Senator from ———." Members, Members-elect, Resident Commissioners, Resident Commissioners-elect, Delegates, and Delegates-elect, may send through the mails, under their franks, within certain limitations, any mail matter to any Government official or to any person, correspondence upon official or departmental business. Retiring Members retain a limited franking privilege during the 90-day period immediately following the day on which they leave office.

27. Are visitors allowed to listen in on the proceedings of Congress?

Yes; both Houses have visitors' galleries. Visitors are subject to control by the Presiding Officers of the two Houses, and the galleries may be cleared in case of disorder. In the Senate Chamber, the galleries are cleared when the Senate goes into executive session. The Legislative Reorganization Act of 1970 makes provisions for the renovation of the House Visitors' Gallery. When completed, the Gallery will be enclosed with a sound-proof transparent cover to eliminate noise. In addition, various devices will be installed to provide explanation to spectators about activities on the House floor. In addition special spaces are set aside for accredited journalists to the Press Gallery, the Radio and TV Gallery, and the Periodical Gallery.

The House is expected to implement a system for television and radio broadcasting of House floor proceedings sometime in 1978. The House voted on October 27, 1977, to empower the Speaker to devise a system for distribution of audio and visual recordings of House proceedings to the broadcast news media. The House vote called on the Speaker to implement this system after receipt, not later than February 15, 1978, of a report by the House Committee on Rules of all alternative methods of providing complete and unedited broadcasting of House floor sessions.

Resolutions providing for the Senate to take similar action have been referred to the Senate Committee on Rules and Administration.

28. How many blacks have served in Congress?

As of December 1977, 45 blacks have served in Congress, 42 in the House and 3 in the Senate. Joseph H. Rainey of South Carolina was the first black to serve in the House, from December 12, 1870 to March 3, 1879. Hiram R. Revels of Mississippi, appointed by the State legislature to fill a vacancy, served in the Senate from February 23, 1870 to March 3, 1871. The Hon. Shirley Chisholm of New York, elected for the first time in 1968, is the first black woman to serve in Congress. William L. Dawson, the first black committee chairman, served as chairman of the House Committee on Government Operations from 1947–1953 and from 1955 until his death in 1970.

29. How many women have served in the Congress; who was the first; how many have chaired committees?

Excluding Delegates, 97 women have been elected or appointed through December 1977: 86 to the House of Representatives only, and 10 to the Senate only. Margaret Chase Smith has served in both the House and Senate. The first woman Member of Congress was Jeanette Rankin who was elected in 1916 before the Nineteenth Amendment guaranteed suffrage to all women. Eight women have chaired congressional committees. Mae Ella Nolan chaired the House Committee on Expenditures in the Post Office Department in the 68th Congress; Mary Theresa Norton chaired the House District of Columbia Committee in the 74th Congress and until June 22, 1937 in the 75th Congress, the House Labor Committee from June 22, 1937 through the 79th Congress, and the House Administration Committee in the 81st Congress; Hattie W. Caraway chaired the Senate Committee on Enrolled Bills in the 73–78th Congresses; Caroline O'Day chaired the Committee on the Election of the President, Vice-President and Representatives in Congress from June 24, 1937 in the 75th Congress, through the end of the 77th Congress; Edith Nourse Rogers chaired the House Veterans' Affairs Committee in the 80th and 83d Congresses; Martha W. Griffiths chaired the Select Committee on the House Beauty Shop from the 90th–93d Congresses; Leonor K. (Mrs. John B.) Sullivan chaired the House Merchant Marine and Fisheries Committee in the 93d and 94th Congresses, and Yvonne B. Burke chaired the Select Committee on the House Beauty Shop in the 94th Congress.

30. Can Members of Congress be impeached?

Probably not. There has been only one case in which proceedings were brought against a Member. He resigned before the case came to trial in the Senate, but the Senate eventually decided it had no jurisdiction. Each House may, by a two-thirds vote, expel a Member, or by a majority vote, may publicly censure a Member. Members of Congress, like private citizens, are subject to prosecution for treason, felony, or breach of the peace.

31. What services are officially available to Members and to committees to assist them in the performance of their legislative duties?

Research assistance for Congress is available through the Office of the Legislative Counsel (one for each House), the Congressional Research Service, the Office of Technology Assessment, the General Accounting Office, and the Congressional Budget Office.

The Legislative Counsel Offices help Members and committees draft bills, resolutions, and amendments and also offer advice on legal problems which arise in connection with a proposal. The Congressional Research Service, located in the Library of Congress, assists Members and committees in analyzing, appraising, and evaluating proposed legislation, and as well assists Members with their constituent inquiries. The Office of Technology Assessment, which began operations in 1973, is authorized to assist committees of the Congress and the House and Senate in assessing the physical, economic, social, or political effects of legislative proposals in order to guard against technological problems which may ensue from legislation passed by the Congress. The General Accounting Office conducts special audits, surveys, and investigations at the request of committees and Members.

The Office of the Law Revision Counsel, established by the Committee Reform Amendments of 1974, is authorized to "develop and keep current an official and positive codification of the laws of the United States," and to recommend "the repeal of obsolete, superfluous, and superceded" public laws.

In addition, each standing committee of the House and Senate is entitled to a staff of professional and clerical employees appointed by majority vote of the committee. Additional committee staff is hired with funds voted to each committee annually. Finally, every Senator and Representative is provided an allotment to hire office staff. Senate and House computer facilities provide substantial assistance to Members, committees, and chamber officers.

House of Representatives

32. Who are the officers of the House, and how are they chosen?

The Constitution (art. I, sec. 2) says that the House "shall choose their Speaker and other officers"—i.e., the membership vote as on any other question, except that in this case it is strictly a party vote. Republicans and Democrats both meet before the House organizes for a new Congress, and choose a slate of officers. These are presented at the initial session of the House, and the majority party slate is selected. The vote is viva voce, except for the Speaker.

The officers include Speaker, Chaplain, Clerk, Sergeant at Arms, Doorkeeper, and Postmaster. Each of these elective officers appoints any employees provided by law for his department. The table on p. 27 shows the party make-up of both the Senate and House of Representatives from the 34th through the 95th Congress.

33. What are the duties of the Speaker of the House?

He presides over the House, appoints the chairmen to preside over the Committees of the Whole, appoints all special or select committees, appoints conference committees, has the power of recognition of Members, has the authority to refer bills to committee, and makes many important rulings and decisions in the House. The Speaker may vote, but usually does not, except in case of a tie. He may participate in debate, but only after relinquishing the chair. The Democrats, when in the majority, have given the Speaker the power to nominate the majority party members of the Rules Committee. The Speaker, along with his party's floor leaders and party organization, determines party policy in the House. The Speaker and the other majority party leaders often confer with the President, and are regarded as spokesmen for the administration if they and the President belong to the same political party.

34. Could a person other than an elected Representative in Congress serve as Speaker of the House?

Yes. There is no constitutional objection to such an arrangement. The House is empowered to choose its Speaker and other officers, without restriction. But in fact, the Speaker has always been a Member of the House.

35. Who has been Speaker of the House of Representatives for the longest period of time?

The late Honorable Sam Rayburn, of Bonham, Texas, who was a Member of the House 48 years and 8 months and served as Speaker 17 years and 2 months. The record for longest continuous service as Speaker is held by John McCormack, of Dorchester, Massachusetts, who served consecutively for 8 years, 11 months, and 23 days, thus surpassing Champ Clark (7 years, 10 months, 29 days) and Joseph G. Cannon (7 years, 3 months, and 24 days).

36. Do the Members of the House have individual seats?

No. They did until the 63d Congress, but now any Member may sit where he chooses. Democrats occupy the east side of the Chamber, on the Speaker's right; Republicans sit across the main aisle on the Speaker's left.

37. What qualifications are prescribed for a Representative in Congress?

A Member of the House of Representatives must be at least 25 years of age, must have been a United States citizen for at least 7 years, and must reside in the State from which he is sent to Congress.

38. What is the size of the House of Representatives and how is it fixed?

The Constitution entitles each State to at least one Representative. Beyond this minimum number, Representatives are apportioned among the States according to population. For the first Congress, i.e., before the taking of the first census, the Constitution itself fixed the number for each State—and therefore the size of the House. The only other constitutional limitation is that the number "shall not exceed one for every thirty Thousand." Within this limit, Congress has the say as to the size of the House. With the great increase in population, and consequent number of Representatives, there have been frequent demands for a smaller House, but to date the trend has been the other way. Under the law now in force, the membership is fixed at 435 indefinitely. In addition to the Representatives from the 50 States there is a Resident Commissioner from Puerto Rico and Delegates from the District of Columbia, the Virgin Islands, and Guam.

39. What is the procedure for apportionment of Representatives?

Population figures used for apportionment of Representatives are determined for States by each decennial census. For many years the actual apportionment was calculated according to the method of "major fractions" but under act of November 15, 1941, Congress adopted the method of "equal proportions." Briefly, this method takes the fixed size (currently 435) and after assigning 1 seat to each State, as required by the Constitution, allots the remaining 385 on the basis of a priority list obtained by dividing the population of each State by the geometric means of successive numbers of Representatives. This method makes the difference between the average number of Representatives per million people in any two States as small as possible.

40. Who defines the congressional districts—the United States or the States?

Congress fixes the size of the House of Representatives, and the procedure for apportioning the number among the States, but the States themselves carry on from there. In the very early years of the Republic, most States elected their Representatives at large. However, the practice of dividing a State into districts was soon instituted. Congress later required that Representatives be elected from "districts composed of a contiguous and compact territory," but this recommendation is no longer in the Federal law.

The actual redistricting process has always been provided for by State law. In 1967, Congress by law prohibited at large elections of Representatives in all States entitled to more than one Representative. Today, all States with more than one Representative must elect heir Representatives from single-member districts.

41. What is the meaning of the phrase "one man, one vote"?

For many years the Supreme Court refused to become involved in redistricting of State legislative or congressional seats. In *Colegrove* v. *Green* (1946) the Court held that such questions were "political" in nature and, therefore, not a proper matter for Court determination.

The Court reversed itself, however, in 1962 when it ruled in *Baker* v. *Carr* that the lower house of the Tennessee State Legislature must be apportioned on the sole basis of population. Within 2 years of this decision suits had been filed in 41 of the 50 States contesting the legitimacy of State or congressional redistrictings. A number of rulings followed including *Wesberry* v. *Sanders* (1964), which held that congressional districts must be composed of substantially equal numbers of people, and *Reynolds* v. *Sims* (1964), which held that in both houses of a bicameral legislature districts must be "as nearly of equal population as is practicable."

The phrase used to describe in a nutshell the Court's requirement for a constitutional redistricting is "one man, one vote," which means that in the drawing of political boundaries for purposes of representation it is essential that a good faith effort be made to attain, as nearly as practicable, equality of population among the districts.

In recent years the Court has held firm to the notion that congressional districts must be substantially equal in population (*White* v. *Weiser*, 1973). Some divergence from a strict population standard in State and local legislatures was allowed in a series of cases including

Mahan v. *Howell* (1973), which permitted a population deviation of 16.4 percent in the size of Virginia State legislative districts. The Court apparently accepted this plan because the Virginia Constitution gives the House of Delegates a strong role in enacting local legislation. This fact persuaded the Court of the legitimacy of Virginia's desire to respect traditional political boundaries in drawing district lines. It is presently unclear how much State legislative district population deviation is acceptable to the Court.

Senate

42. What qualifications are prescribed for a Member of the Senate?

A member of the United States Senate must be at least 30 years of age, must have been a citizen of the United States for 9 years, and must be a resident of the State from which he is sent to Congress.

43. Does the term "senior Senator" apply to age or service?

The word "senior" or "junior" as applied to Senators refers to their service, and not to their ages. A "senior Senator" may be much younger in years than the "junior Senator." A Senator must have served continuously to be entitled to the senior rank, which also carries a little more prestige with the Senate body and the administration.

44. Have U.S. Senators always been elected by the people?

Senators were originally elected by the State legislatures (Constitution, art. I, sec. 3). Direct election by the people was provided for by the 17th amendment, effective as to Senators elected after May 31, 1913.

45. In the event of the death or resignation of a U.S. Senator, how is the vacancy filled?

A vacancy in the office of United States Senator from any State is usually filled by a temporary appointment by the governor, which continues until the general election, at which time a Senator is elected for the remainder of the term, if it had longer to run. The 17th amendment directs the governor to call an election, but authorizes the legislatures to make provision for an immediate appointment pending election, and this alternative is ordinarily followed.

46. Do Senators have individual seats assigned them?

Yes. The individual seats are numbered and assigned on request of Senators in order of their seniority. Democrats occupy the west side of the Chamber—on the Vice President's right; Republicans sit across the main aisle to his left. There is no set rule for the seating of "independents."

47. Who are the officers of the Senate and how are they chosen?

The Constitution provides that the Vice President of the United States shall be the President of the Senate. The Senate also elects by resolution a President *pro tempore* who is a Member who presides during absences of the Vice President. Former Vice Presidents serving in the Senate are accorded the honorary title of Deputy President *pro tempore* of the Senate.

Other officers chosen by resolution are the Secretary, Sergeant at Arms, Chaplain, Secretary for the Majority, and Secretary for the Minority.

48. Can the Vice President vote in the Senate?

He can do so only in the event of a tie vote.

49. Does the President pro tempore vote in the Senate?

Yes. He participates in Senate debates and votes.

Organization and Procedure

50. How are the rules of procedure in Congress determined?

The Constitution provides that each House may determine the rules of its proceedings.

51. What is a party leader?

There is a majority leader and a minority leader. In talks on the floor, Members do not usually refer to Democrats and Republicans. Generally, they refer to the "majority" and the "minority."

The leader is all the title implies. He leads in party debate. He brings forward party programs and policies. His advocacy of, or opposition to, proposed legislation indicates the party preference. The majority leader has much control over what legislative programs come up and when.

52. Is the majority leader, in either branch of Congress, elected by the House or Senate?

The majority leaders in both House and Senate are not officers of that body, but of the party numerically in the majority at the time. So while each House, under the Constitution, chooses its officers, majority leaders are not selected by the House or Senate as such but by a party caucus or conference.

53. What are the duties of the "whips" of the Congress?

The whips (of the majority and minority parties) keep track of all important political legislation and endeavor to have all members of their parties present when important measures are to be voted upon. When the vote is likely to be close they check up, find out who is out of the city, and advise absentees by wire of the important measures coming up.

The office of whip is unofficial and carries no special salary. Each whip, however, is allowed certain additional help, sufficient office space, and to incur additional expenses in the performance of his duties.

54. Do the political parties offer legislative guidance to their individual Members in Congress?

The Democratic and Republican parties try to guide their Members by means of caucuses and conferences. The party caucus or conference is the organizational body of all party Members in the House or Senate, and is additionally responsible for selecting the party's leaders, candidates for various official posts in the House or Senate, and for approving Members' appointments to House or Senate standing committees. The caucus or conference serves as a forum for all party members to discuss pending legislation.

The House Democratic Caucus may also, by majority vote, instruct Democratic members of House committees or House Democrats on joint committees, to vote in a particular fashion with respect to legislation or other matters pending before their committees.

In recent years, a variety of informal member organizations have been formed to provide interested members with legislative and policy information on a wide variety of issues. These groups differ from the formal caucus or conference in that informal groups are not recognized in the *Rules* of either House, and that informal group membership is entirely voluntary.

55. What are the powers and duties of the Sergeants at Arms of the Senate and House of Representatives?

The office of Sergeant at Arms is derived from a similar office in both Houses of the British Parliament. The Sergeant at Arms is, above all, the chief disciplinary officer and is empowered to enforce order upon the floor. In the House he has a special symbol of office, the mace; also, he is the disbursing officer for Members' salary and mileage. Both officers share certain joint responsibilities, such as policing the Capitol and grounds; they act as executive and purchasing officers for their respective bodies, and in general see to it that the respective rules and wishes of the two Houses are faithfully carried out. Finally, in each House, its Sergeant at Arms, by the direction of the Presiding Officer, may compel the attendance of absent Members.

56. What are the duties of the Parliamentarians?

Both the House and the Senate appoint a Parliamentarian to assist in rendering correct parliamentary decisions and to keep the practices and precedents uniform. He must be so well versed with the rules and practices of his House that he can give the Chair a decision on a moment's notice.

57. Does a President have any control over the sessions of Congress?

Under the Constitution, the President may convene Congress, or either House, "on extraordinary occasions." It is usual for the President in calling an extra session to indicate the exact matter which needs the attention of Congress. However, once convened, a Congress cannot be limited in the subject matter which it will consider.

The President is also empowered by the Constitution to adjourn Congress "at such times as he may think proper" when the House and Senate disagree with respect to the time for adjournment. No President has exercised this power. Many constitutional experts believe the provision applies only in the case of extraordinary sessions.

58. When Congress is in session, at what hour do the two Houses meet?

The time of meeting is fixed by each House. Under standing order, the House ordinarily meets at 12 o'clock noon and usually remains in session until 5 or 6 p.m.

The Senate also ordinarily meets at "12 o'clock meridian." No reason is known for this wording in the Senate, which calls it meridian rather than noon.

59. What are the customary proceedings when the House meets?

The Speaker calls the Members to order, and the Sergeant at Arms places the mace on the pedestal at the right of the Speaker's platform. Then the Chaplain offers prayers. Next the Speaker announces his approval of the *Journal* for the preceding day's activities without its having to be read, unless he orders that it be read or a motion to read it is passed. Members of the committee make reports of bills and then the House is ready to consider the bills left unfinished the day before or to take up a new bill on the Calendar, if there is no unfinished business.

60. What is a quorum of the House?

In the House of Representatives a quorum is a majority of the membership. When there are no vacancies in the membership a quorum is 218. There are usually a few vacancies—Members who have died or have resigned and their places yet unfilled. So an actual quorum is usually a little under that figure. Much business is transacted without a quorum. But no business of any importance, except to adjourn, can be transacted without a quorum present if any Member objects. All any Member has to do to get a full House is to arise, address the Speaker, and make a point of order that "no quorum is present." The Speaker says, "The Chair will count." If he cannot count a quorum present, the doors are closed, the bells are rung in the corridors and House Office Buildings (three rings indicate a call of the House), and the roll is called. This usually produces a quorum and business proceeds.

A majority of the membership also constitutes a quorum to do business in the Senate.

61. What business can be transacted by unanimous consent?

Practically anything can be done in either House by unanimous consent—except where the Constitution or the rules specifically prohibit the Presiding Officer from entertaining such a request. For example, since the Constitution requires that a rollcall vote be taken to pass a bill over a presidential veto, the Presiding Officer of the House or the Senate cannot entertain a unanimous-consent request to waive this requirement; in the House of Representatives, the Presiding Officer cannot admit to the Chamber persons who are not permitted to be present under the rules; nor may visitors in the galleries be introduced to the House. A majority of bills are passed by unanimous consent.

62. Has the Congress ever altered its methods of organization and procedure?

Congressional organization and procedure have been changed many times in the past.

In the early years, there were very few standing committees in the House—only six in 1800. The work was done by the House in general session, and by numerous special committees created to handle specific problems. The standing committees developed gradually during the first half of the nineteenth century. The Speaker eventually gained power until by the early years of this century he was regarded as second only to the President in the power of his office. In rules changes adopted in 1910 and 1911, the Speaker was denied his traditional chairmanship of the powerful Rules Committee as well as the power of appointing standing committees.

In 1917, the Senate adopted the "rule of cloture" which made it possible to end debate on a measure by a two-thirds vote. The cloture rule was amended in 1959 to again permit two-thirds of the Senators voting to close off debate (the 1949 Wherry amendment had required two-thirds of the entire Senate membership to invoke cloture). The cloture rule was further amended in 1975 to permit three-fifths of the entire Senate membership to close off debate.

The Legislative Reorganization Act of 1946 significantly changed the rules and organization of both the House and Senate. It also reduced the number of standing committees in both Houses. The 1970 Legislative Reorganization Act also provided for changes in congressional procedure.

The Committee Reform Amendments of 1974 refined House committee jurisdictions, required expanded congressional oversight of the executive branch, and modified committee procedures.

In 1977, the Senate passed S. Res. 4, the Senate Committee System Reorganization Amendments. This measure consolidated and redefined the jurisdictions of Senate committees, revised Senators' committee service limitations, established for the first time subcommittee service limitations, recommended establishment of a computerized committee meeting scheduling system, and adopted revised procedures for the referral of complex legislation to more than one committee.

63. What are the stages of a bill in the House?

Following in brief are the usual steps in procedure—further details on some of the stages are presented in subsequent paragraphs:

(a) Introduction by a Member, by placing the measure in the "hopper," a box on the clerk's desk; it is numbered and sent to the Government Printing Office and made available next morning at the document room.

(b) Reference to a standing or select committee—public bills and bills coming from the Senate, by the Parliamentarian under direction of the Speaker, private bills on endorsement of the Member.

(c) Report from committee—usually after hearing, either before the full commitee or a subcommittee.

(d) Placing on the calendar—according to its classification as a revenue bill, private bill, etc. Occasionally a privileged bill is considered when reported.

(e) Consideration in Committee of the Whole, if on the Union Calendar—including general debate and reading for amendments, with speeches limited to 5 minutes for and against amendments.

(f) Second reading and consideration in the House—in the case of bills considered in Committee of the Whole, the second reading is had in Committee. In either case, the bill is open to amendment on the second reading.

(g) Engrossment and third reading—the question is put by the Speaker as a matter of course and decided at one vote. Any Member may demand reading in full. A negative vote at this stage defeats the bill as completely as a vote on passage.

(*h*) Passage—the question of the passage being put by the Speaker as a matter of course without motion from the floor.

(*i*) Transmission to the Senate, by message.

(*j*) Consideration by the Senate—usually after reference to and report from committee, reading, debate, and opportunity for amendment.

(*k*) Return from Senate with or without amendment—if the Senate rejects the House bill it so notifies the House.

(*l*) Consideration of Senate amendments by the House—either agreeing, agreeing with amendment, or disagreeing with each amendment separately.

(*m*) Settlement of differences by conference.

(*n*) Enrollment on parchment paper.

(*o*) Examination by the appropriate committee—the chairmen of the House and Senate committees each certifying as to the correctness of the enrollment of bills of their respective bodies.

(*p*) Signing—by the Speaker first in all cases, then by the President of the Senate.

(*q*) Transmittal to the President of the United States.

(*r*) Approval or disapproval by the President—usually after referring it to the department affected for recommendation.

(*s*) Action on a bill vetoed—the House or Senate may consider the veto message at once, postpone consideration of the message to a certain day, or refer the same to a committee. If it fails to pass the House to which returned, by a two-thirds vote, no further action is taken.

(*t*) Filing with the Administrator of General Services on approval or passage over veto.

64. How do Members of Congress introduce bills?

When a Senator rises to introduce a bill, he says, "Mr. President," and waits for the Vice President to recognize him. The Vice President recognizes the Senator by looking at him and saying: "The Senator from * * * ," naming the State from which the Senator comes.

Then the Senator states that he desires to introduce a bill.

A Senator often introduces several bills at the same time by saying that he desires to introduce sundry bills and have them referred to the proper committees. A Senator may introduce a bill at any time by obtaining unanimous consent for that purpose.

Members of the House introduce bills by placing them in a "hopper," a box on the Clerk's desk.

65. What is the first reading of a bill?

Formerly a bill was first read by title at the time of introduction. Since 1890, the first reading is accomplished by the mere printing of the title in the *Congressional Record* and the *Journal*.

66. What is meant by the different calendars of the House?

A legislative calendar is a docket or list of measures reported from committee and ready for consideration by the House. There are three calendars to which business reported from committees is initially referred:

1. A calendar of the Committee of the Whole House on the State of the Union, frequently called the Union Calendar, to which are

referred all public bills raising revenue or involving a charge against the Government.

2. A House Calendar, for all public bills not raising revenue or appropriating money or property.

3. A calendar of the Committee of the Whole House for all private bills—the so-called Private Calendar.

There is also a special calendar, known as the Consent Calendar, to which measures may be referred on request of a Member from either the Union or the House Calendar. Bills on this calendar are called in the order in which they appear. Consideration is blocked by a single objection; and when it is again called on the calendar, if three Members object, it is stricken from the Consent Calendar.

67. What are the functions of the House Rules Committee?

This committee expedites House consideration of bills reported by other committees. Most of its work is to decide whether or not to grant special consideration for bills which otherwise might be long delayed on the various calendars of the House. When the Rules Committee reports a special rule to the House, it is usually adopted. When it is adopted, the bill to which it refers is considered under the provisions of that rule.

68. What is the Committee of the Whole?

Motions or propositions involving taxes or appropriations, authorizing payments out of appropriations or releasing liability to the United States or referring claims to the Court of Claims, are considered first in the House sitting as a Committee of the Whole. (There are technically two such committees, in effect standing committees—one, the Committee of the Whole House, to consider business on the Private Calendar, and the other, the Committee of the Whole House on the State of the Union, to consider business on the Union Calendar.) Upon resolving into Committee of the Whole, the Speaker gives way to a Chairman appointed by him and the mace is moved to a lower pedestal. Speeches are limited to 5 minutes for and against amendments. The "previous question" cannot be put in the Committee; and the Committee does not adjourn, but rises and reports to the House, whether their business is unfinished or finished. A quorum is 100 Members.

The Senate in 1930 discontinued the device of a Committee of the Whole except in considering treaties.

69. How do Members obtain permission to speak?

The Rules of the House prescribe the following: "When any Member means to speak, he is to stand up in his place * * * and address himself, not to the House or any particular Member, but to the Speaker * * *"

In the Senate, a Member stands, addresses the Presiding Officer, and does not proceed until he is recognized. The Presiding Officer, in turn, is required to recognize the Senator who first addressed him.

70. Are there time limitations on debate in Congress?

The term "filibuster" is used to describe delaying tactics which are designed to prevent action on a measure in legislative bodies. Filibusters are not possible in the House because no Member is permitted to speak for longer than one hour without unanimous consent. Moreover, in the House, a majority can call for the "previous question" and bring a bill to an immediate vote.

In the Senate, a Member can filibuster without speaking continuously; he may yield to a colleague for a question, or call a quorum without losing the floor. In the event a recess is called, he is entitled to regain the floor when the Senate reassembles.

In 1917, the Senate adopted the cloture rule. As amended in 1975, it provides that the Senate may end debate on a pending bill by a three-fifths vote of the entire Senate membership. When 16 Senators file a petition asking to end debate, the Senate must vote on the petition at 1 p.m. of the second calendar day thereafter. If three-fifths of the Senate votes for cloture, then no Senator may thereafter talk longer than 1 hour. So long as fewer than 60 Senators are opposed to cloture, it is impossible to end a filibuster if enough of those Senators are willing to talk in relays. On measures changing the Senate rules, the support of two-thirds of the Senators present and voting is required to bring debate to a close.

71. What is the "previous question"?

A motion for the previous question, if agreed to by a majority of Members voting, has the effect of cutting off all debate and bringing the House to a direct vote upon the immediate question or questions on which it has been asked and ordered. The Senate has no previous question rule.

72. How are record votes taken in the Congress?

The Constitution provides that "the yeas and nays of the Members of either House on any question shall, at the desire of one-fifth of those present, be entered on the Journal."

Most votes are generally taken by a simple voice method. The House, prior to 1970, did not permit recorded votes in Committee of the Whole where most of its floor action occurs. However, the Legislative Reorganization Act of 1970 provided for recorded votes in Committee of the Whole. In 1973, the House installed an electronic voting device to reduce the time consumed in voting.

73. What is pairing?

In the House, a pair is a written agreement between Members on opposite sides not to vote on a specified question (a "live" pair) or during a stipulated time (a "general" pair). In effect, it is equivalent to a vote on the part of each against the proposition favored by his colleague. The practice appeared in the House as early as 1824. It was not officially recognized in the House rules until 1880. Pairs are announced by the Clerk and published in the *Record*.

Pairing is also practiced and permitted in the Senate although not recognized by the rules.

74. What is the difference between an "engrossed" and an "enrolled" bill?

Engrossing a bill is a means of identification. An engrossed Senate bill is printed on white paper; a House initiated bill is engrossed on blue paper. The engrossing is ordered along with the third, and final, reading of a bill.

When a bill has passed both House and Senate, the second House to take action notifies the first that the measure has passed; the originating House then causes the bill to be "enrolled" on parchment. When printed in this form, there are no breaks or paragraphs in the flow of the language of the bill. The purpose of inscribing the bill solidly is to insure insufficient space between paragraphs for forgery.

75. How many types of resolutions can Congress pass?

There are three kinds of resolutions acted upon by Congress: a simple resolution, which is passed by one House only; a concurrent resolution, which must pass both Houses; and a joint resolution, which requires the action of both Houses and signature of the President unless it is a proposed amendment to the Constitution.

76. What is meant by a public bill (or law)?

A bill dealing with classes of citizens is a public bill as distinguished from a private bill for the benefit of individuals. It is not always obvious whether a bill is public or private; for example, a bill for the benefit of individuals, but which included provisions of general legislation, was classed as a public bill. The question comes up chiefly in determining whether the bill should be referred to the Union, House, or the Private Calendar—and whether the resulting law should be printed in part 1 (public laws) or part 2 (private laws) of the *Statutes at Large*.

77. What is the difference between a bill and an act?

"Bill" is the technical designation of a measure introduced in either House, and until it has been passed by that House. At that point it is reprinted as an act, i.e., an act of one branch of the Congress. The term "act" is, however, popularly used in referring to a measure which has been finally passed by both Houses and becomes law, whether by approval of the President or by passage over his veto.

78. What is the largest number of bills and joint resolutions ever introduced in a single Congress?

In the 61st Congress (1909–11), there was a total of 44,363 such measures introduced in both Houses. Around 25,000 bills and joint resolutions are introduced in the average Congress.

79. How does the total of bills and joint resolutions introduced in Congress compare with the number enacted?

From March 4, 1789, to the adjournment of the 94th Congress, 1,084,147 bills and joint resolutions have been introduced in both Houses. Of this total, only 87,620 were enacted.

80. What courses are open to the President when a bill is presented to him?

(a) The President may promptly sign it, whereupon it becomes a law. (b) He may hold it, without taking any action, in which case it becomes law at the expiration of 10 days (Sundays excepted) without his signature if Congress is in session. (He may refuse to sign the bill because he disapproves of the measure and recognizes that a veto is either politically unwise or useless, or because he is undecided about the bill's constitutionality, as was President Cleveland on the income tax law of 1894, and prefers not to commit himself.) (c) He may veto the bill. In this case, it may be voted on again by Congress—if it is in session—and if approved by a two-thirds vote in both Houses, it becomes law despite the President's veto.

81. What is a "veto"?

The word "veto" is derived from the Latin and means "I forbid." The President is authorized by the Constitution to refuse his assent to any measure presented by Congress for his approval. In such case, he returns the measure to the House in which it originated, at the same time indicating his objections—the so-called veto message. The veto goes to the entire measure; the President is not authorized, as are the Governors of some States, to veto separate items in a bill.

82. What is a "pocket veto"?

By the Constitution the President is allowed 10 days (exclusive of Sundays) from the date of receiving a bill within which to give it his approval; if, within 10 days, Congress adjourns and so prevents the return of a bill to which the President objects, that bill does not become law. In many cases, where bills have been sent to him toward the close of a session, the President has taken advantage of this provision, and has held until after adjournment measures of which he disapproved but which for some reason he did not wish to return with his objections to Congress for their further action. This action is the so-called pocket veto.

83. What important court cases have related to the pocket veto?

In *The Pocket Veto Case* (279 U.S. 655, 1929) the Supreme Court decided that when Congress had adjourned at the close of a first regular session—not to reassemble, perhaps, for several months—it had effectively prevented the return of a bill which the President had vetoed, and that the bill in such case did not become law.

In *Wright* v. *U.S.* (302 U.S. 583, 1938) the Court decided that in the case of a temporary recess by one House only, while Congress was still in session, the President could constitutionally return a vetoed bill to the proper officer of the House, which could then take what action it saw fit.

In *Kennedy* v. *Sampson*, a 1974 D.C. United States Court of Appeals' decision, the court held that President Nixon had erred in declaring a bill pocket vetoed December 24 because a congressional recess from December 22 to December 28 prevented his returning the bill to the Congress. The court declared that Congress had made arrangements for deliverance of presidential messages to it and so the President had sources to whom he could deliver a regular veto message. It further found that when Congress is absent during intrasession recesses but will be returning, it deserves the opportunity to override a veto. Accordingly, Presidents may no longer use an intrasession recess to pocket veto bills and thus avoid a possible reversal in Congress. The Justice Department failed to appeal this decision to the Supreme Court, although it has expressed its opinion that the court's ruling is not binding, and that Senator Kennedy, who initiated the suit, had no legal standing to do so.

84. Are many bills vetoed?

As of December 31, 1977, Presidents of the United States had vetoed 2,361 acts of Congress. Woodrow Wilson, in 8 years, vetoed

44 bills. President Harding vetoed 6; Coolidge, 50; and Hoover, 37. President Cleveland vetoed more bills than any other President before Franklin Roosevelt, but the bills were mostly private pension bills.

During Cleveland's 2 terms, he vetoed 584 bills (238 of these were pocket vetoes). During Franklin D. Roosevelt's administration of 12 years, 1 month, and 8 days, he vetoed 635 bills (263 of them being pocket vetoes). President Truman vetoed 250 bills, 70 of which were pocket vetoes, from April 12, 1945, to January 20, 1953. President Eisenhower vetoed 181 bills, 108 of them pocket vetoes, during his 2 terms. President Kennedy vetoed 21 bills, including 9 pocket vetoes. President Johnson vetoed 30 bills, including 14 pocket vetoes. President Nixon vetoed 43 bills, including 17 pocket vetoes. President Ford vetoed 66 bills, including 18 pocket vetoes. As of December 31, 1977, President Carter had vetoed two bills.

85. Are bills often passed over the President's veto?

Not very often. In the entire history of our country, as of December 31, 1977, only 90 bills have been enacted by overriding a veto. Of these, 15 were passed over the veto of President Andrew Johnson; 12 each over the vetoes of Presidents Truman and Ford; 9 over the veto of Franklin D. Roosevelt; 7 over the veto of President Cleveland; 6 over the veto of Woodrow Wilson; 5 over the vetoes of Presidents Pierce and Nixon; 4 over the vetoes of Presidents Grant and Coolidge; 3 over the veto of President Hoover; 2 over the veto of President Eisenhower; and 1 bill was passed over the vetoes of Presidents Tyler, Hayes, Arthur, Benjamin Harrison, Theodore Roosevelt, and Taft, respectively.

86. When does a bill, introduced at the beginning of a Congress, become "dead" and no longer open to consideration?

A bill introduced at any time during a Congress may be considered until the close of that Congress, irrespective of sessions. Thus, a bill introduced in January 1975, would, barring other considerations, be subject to action by the House until the final adjournment *sine die* of the 94th Congress.

87. What becomes of a bill after it is signed?

A signed bill is sent to the General Services Administration. There it is given a number as a public law and published forthwith as a "slip law"—i.e., in individual form. At the close of each session these are consolidated in a bound volume called *United States Statutes at Large*.

All of the permanent laws of the United States of general application currently in force are included in the *Code of the Laws of the United States of America*. The *Code* and annual supplements, in the past published under the supervision of the Committee on the Judiciary of the House of Representatives, printed at the Government Printing Office, and available from the Superintendent of Documents, are now the responsibility of the Office of Law Revision Counsel.

88. What is the role of the Congress in the impeachment process?

Impeachment is the process by which the President, Vice President, Federal judges, and all civil officials of the United States may be removed from office. Officials may be impeached for treason, bribery, and other high crimes and misdemeanors.

The House of Representatives has the sole authority to bring charges of impeachment (by a simple majority vote), and the Senate has the sole authority to try impeachment charges. An official may be removed from office only upon conviction, which requires a two-thirds vote of the Senate. The Constitution provides that the Chief Justice shall preside when the President is being tried for impeachment.

89. Why must tax bills originate in the House?

The constitutional provision (all bills for raising revenue shall originate in the House of Representatives; art. I, sec. 7) is an adaptation of the English practice. The principle involved, which had been established in England after long struggle, is that the national purse strings should be controlled by a body directly responsible to the people. So when the Constitution was formulated, as Members of the Senate were to be chosen by the several State legislatures, the initiation of revenue legislation was restricted to the House, where the Members were subject to direct election every 2 years. However, the Senate has had from the start full power to amend revenue legislation.

90. Must all appropriation bills originate in the House?

There has been considerable argument and difference of opinion as to whether "bills for raising revenue" include appropriation bills. But it is uniform practice that general appropriation, as distinguished from special bills appropriating for single, specific purposes, originate in the House.

91. What is a deficiency, or supplemental, bill?

A deficiency bill, now called a supplemental, is one carrying appropriations to supplement appropriations which have proved insufficient. Appropriations are normally made on the basis of estimates for a year but conditions may arise which exhaust the appropriations before October 1.

92. What is meant by a "rider" on a congressional bill?

A "rider" is an extraneous provision incorporated in an appropriation bill, with the idea of its "riding" through to enactment on the merits of the main measure. The practice is very old; in 1837 a "rider" on the fortifications appropriations bill would have provided for the disposal of the surplus funds in the Treasury. Under the rules any item of appropriation in a general appropriation bill that is not authorized by existing law nor in furtherance of projects already in progress is subject to a point of order (this is often waived by a special rule in the House); and the same with any provision "changing existing law," unless it is germane to the subject and designed to retrench expenditures (the so-called Holman rule). Occasionally a "rider" becomes law, without the point of order being raised.

An example of a legislative rider was contained in an appropriation rescission bill which was vetoed by President Truman. The rider, which was not germane to the bill and wholly unrelated to its subject matter, provided that the United States Employment Service would be returned to the States in 100 days.

President Truman, believing that this subject should receive separate consideration and was entitled to be passed upon by him separate and distinct from any other legislation, vetoed the entire bill to get rid of the rider.

93. What is "lobbying"?

In the broadest sense, this is any activity which has as its ultimate aim to influence the decisions of Congress, State and local legislatures, or executive agencies. The term arose from the use of lobbies, or corridors, in legislative halls as places to meet with and persuade legislators to vote a certain way. Lobbying in general is not an evil; many lobbies provide legislatures with reliable firsthand information of considerable value. But some lobbies have given the practice an undesirable connotation.

94. What Congressional regulations are imposed upon lobbyists?

The Federal Regulation of Lobbying Act of 1946 requires that persons who solicit or accept contributions for lobbying purposes, keep accounts, present receipts and statements to the Clerk of the House, and register with the Clerk of the House and the Secretary of the Senate. The information received is published quarterly in the *Congressional Record*. The purpose of this registration is to disclose the sponsorship and source of funds of lobbyists, but not to curtail the right of persons to act as lobbyists.

The Committee System

95. Why are congressional standing committees necessary?

Standing committees were established as early as 1803; before that, bills were discussed in Committee of the Whole, and then referred to a select committee for drafting. The development of standing committees of small membership (the largest in the House, Appropriations, has 55 members) was a practical necessity to ensure a preliminary check on the flood of bills introduced. Committee procedure, with its witnesses and cross-examination, offers a much more satisfactory method of reaching the real merits of a measure and presenting it in workable form than the necessarily limited consideration on the floor by a (possible) membership of 435.

96. How are the members of the standing committees selected?

Both parties have a committee on committees to recommend committee assignments subject to caucus approval. The proportion of Republicans to Democrats is fixed by the party in the majority for the time being. The House, then, by strict party vote, adopts the slate presented by the two parties. A similar method is used in the Senate.

97. What are the standing committees of the Senate?

The 15 standing committees are as follows: Agriculture, Nutrition, and Forestry; Appropriations; Armed Services; Banking, Housing, and Urban Affairs; Budget; Commerce, Science, and Transportation; Energy and Natural Resources; Environment and Public Works; Finance; Foreign Relations; Governmental Affairs; Human Resources; Judiciary; Rules and Administration; Veterans' Affairs.

98. What constitutes a quorum of a standing committee of the Senate?

Each Senate committee is authorized to establish a quorum for transaction of business—not less (except for taking testimony) than one-third the membership of the committee. A majority of the committee must be present to report a bill or recommendation.

99. What are the standing committees of the House?

There are 22 standing committees as follows: Agriculture; Appropriations; Armed Services; Banking, Finance, and Urban Affairs; Budget; District of Columbia; Education and Labor; Government Operations; House Administration; Interior and Insular Affairs; International Relations; Interstate and Foreign Commerce; Judiciary; Merchant Marine and Fisheries; Post Office and Civil Service; Public Works and Transportation; Rules; Science and Technology; Small Business; Standards of Official Conduct; Veterans' Affairs; and Ways and Means.

100. What is meant by the "seniority rule"?

It is the custom whereby a Member who has served longest on the majority side of a committee becomes its chairman. Members are ranked from the chairmanship according to length of service on the committee. If a Member loses his seat in Congress, and then returns, he starts at the bottom of the list again, except that he outranks those Members who are beginning their first terms. Modifications made in the 92d, 93d, and 94th Congresses have caused the seniority rule to be less rigidly followed than in previous years.

101. Under what circumstances do committees originate bills?

Members sometimes present petitions. Reference of such petition to the committee having jurisdiction of the subject matter gives it authority to draw a bill. The same is true when communications addressed to the Congress from the President, executive departments, or other sources are referred to appropriate committees. General supply bills, revenue measures, and other similar proposals originate in the committees.

102. Do the congressional committees hold hearings on all bills referred to them?

It is the view of many committees that any Member who insists on a hearing on any bill should have it. But there may be several bills almost identical or similar in substance. In such cases hearings frequently are on a group of related measures, or a hearing held on one bill serves for all. It is not always possible for a Member to have a hearing on his bill before a committee because of the tremendous pressure of business.

103. Are committee hearings open to the public?

Hearings by House committees and subcommittees are open to the public except when a committee, by majority vote, determines otherwise.

The Legislative Reorganization Act of 1970 permits, for the first time, radio and television broadcast of House committee and subcommittee hearings but only if a majority of the committee so votes and only if decorum is observed in their broadcast.

Hearings by Senate committees and subcommittees are also open to the public. Senate committee hearings may be closed to the public if the committee determines that testimony to be taken may relate to national security, reflect adversely on the character or reputation of witnesses, or divulge information which is of a confidential nature.

Hearings in the Senate have been broadcast for a number of years.

104. Does the congressional committee to which a bill is referred effectively control its disposition?

Ordinarily the action of a committee in failing to report a measure spells its defeat in either House. However, the House rules provide machinery by which a public bill may be taken out of committee, if held longer than 30 days. A petition, signed by a majority of the membership (218 Members), to discharge a committee from further consideration of the bill, will be placed on a special calendar and may be called up by any of the signers on the second or fourth Monday of any month. Only 20 minutes' debate is allowed on the motion; if it prevails, then the House further votes to consider the bill. It is then considered under the general rules.

This special procedure is resorted to very infrequently, and usually on measures of a controversial character. This is the House machinery for forcing consideration of measures which may be "buried" in committee. It is also possible to discharge a Senate committee by motion, but it is rarely done.

105. What is a select committee?

A select committee is one established by the House or Senate usually for a limited period and generally for a strictly temporary purpose. When that function has been carried out the select committee automatically expires. A standing committee, on the other hand, is a regular, permanent unit in Congress.

106. What are joint committees and how are they established?

Joint committees are those which have members chosen from both the House and Senate, generally with the chairmanship rotating between the most senior majority party Senator and Representative. These committees can be created by statute, or by joint or concurrent resolution. However, all existing joint committees have been established by statute, the oldest being the Joint Committee on the Library which dates from 1800.

107. What is a conference committee?

From the earliest days, differences of opinion between the two Houses have been committed to conference committees to work out a settlement. The most usual case is that in which a bill passes one House with amendments unacceptable to the other. In such a case, the House which disagrees to the amendments generally asks for a conference, and the Speaker (and the Vice President for the Senate), appoints the "managers," as the conferees are called. Generally they are selected from the committee having charge of the bill and they usually represent majority and minority positions on the bill. After attempting to resolve the points in disagreement, the conference committee issues a report to each House. If the report is accepted by both Houses, the bill is then signed and sent to the President. If rejected by either House, the matter in disagreement comes up for disposition anew as if there had been no conference. Unless all differences between the Houses are finally adjusted, the bill fails.

Traditionally, conference committees meet in executive sessions closed to the public. However, recent efforts by the Congress have resulted in open conference committee sessions, with only a few conferences being closed for security, and other, reasons.

POLITICAL DIVISIONS OF THE U.S. SENATE AND HOUSE OF REPRESENTATIVES FROM 1855 (34TH CONG.) TO 1977–79 (95TH CONG.)

[All figures reflect immediate result of elections]

Congress		Senate					House of Representatives				
		Number of Senators	Democrats	Republicans	Other parties	Vacant	Number of Representatives	Democrats	Republicans	Other parties	Vacant
34th	1855–1857	62	42	15	5	....	234	83	108	43	....
35th	1857–1859	64	39	20	5	....	237	131	92	14	....
36th	1859–1861	66	38	26	2	....	237	101	113	23	....
37th	1861–1863	50	11	31	7	1	178	42	106	28	2
38th	1863–1865	51	12	39	....	....	183	80	103	....	....
39th	1865–1867	52	10	42	....	....	191	46	145	....	....
40th	1867–1869	53	11	42	....	....	193	49	143	....	1
41st	1869–1871	74	11	61	....	2	243	73	170	....	....
42d	1871–1873	74	17	57	....	....	243	104	139	....	....
43d	1873–1875	74	19	54	....	1	293	88	203	....	2
44th	1875–1877	76	29	46	....	1	293	181	107	3	2
45th	1877–1879	76	36	39	1	....	293	156	137	....	....
46th	1879–1881	76	43	33	....	....	293	150	128	14	1
47th	1881–1883	76	37	37	2	....	293	130	152	11	....
48th	1883–1885	76	36	40	....	....	325	200	119	6	....
49th	1885–1887	76	34	41	....	1	325	182	140	2	1
50th	1887–1889	76	37	39	....	....	325	170	151	4	....
51st	1889–1891	84	37	47	....	....	330	156	173	1	....
52d	1891–1893	88	39	47	2	....	333	231	88	14	....
53d	1893–1895	88	44	38	3	3	356	220	126	10	....
54th	1895–1897	88	39	44	5	....	357	104	246	7	....
55th	1897–1899	90	34	46	10	....	357	134	206	16	1
56th	1899–1901	90	26	53	11	....	357	163	185	9	....
57th	1901–1903	90	29	56	3	2	357	153	198	5	1
58th	1903–1905	90	32	58	....	....	386	178	207	....	1
59th	1905–1907	90	32	58	....	....	386	136	250	....	....
60th	1907–1909	92	29	61	....	2	386	164	222	....	....
61st	1909–1911	92	32	59	....	1	391	172	219	....	....
62d	1911–1913	92	42	49	....	1	391	228	162	1	....
63d	1913–1915	96	51	44	1	....	435	290	127	18	....
64th	1915–1917	96	56	39	1	....	435	231	193	8	3
65th	1917–1919	96	53	42	1	....	435	[1] 210	216	9	....
66th	1919–1921	96	47	48	1	....	435	191	237	7	....
67th	1921–1923	96	37	59	....	....	435	132	300	1	2
68th	1923–1925	96	43	51	2	....	435	207	225	3	....
69th	1925–1927	96	40	54	1	1	435	183	247	5	....
70th	1927–1929	96	47	48	1	....	435	195	237	3	....
71st	1929–1931	96	39	56	1	....	435	163	267	1	4
72d	1931–1933	96	47	48	1	....	435	[2] 216	218	1	....
73d	1933–1935	96	59	36	1	....	435	313	117	5	....
74th	1935–1937	96	69	25	2	....	435	322	103	10	....
75th	1937–1939	96	75	17	4	....	435	333	89	13	....
76th	1939–1941	96	69	23	4	....	435	262	169	4	....
77th	1941–1943	96	66	28	2	....	435	267	162	6	....
78th	1943–1945	96	57	38	1	....	435	222	209	4	....
79th	1945–1947	96	57	38	1	....	435	243	190	2	....
80th	1947–1949	96	45	51	....	....	435	188	246	1	....
81st	1949–1951	96	54	42	....	....	435	263	171	1	....
82d	1951–1953	96	48	47	1	....	435	234	199	2	....
83d	1953–1955	96	46	48	2	....	435	213	221	1	....
84th	1955–1957	96	48	47	1	....	435	232	203	....	....
85th	1957–1959	96	49	47	....	....	435	234	201	....	....
86th	1959–1961	98	64	34	....	....	[3] 436	283	153	....	....
87th	1961–1963	100	64	36	....	....	[4] 437	262	175	....	....
88th	1963–1965	100	67	33	....	....	435	258	176	....	1
89th	1965–1967	100	68	32	....	....	435	295	140	....	....
90th	1967–1969	100	64	36	....	....	435	248	187	....	....
91st	1969–1971	100	58	42	....	....	435	243	192	....	....
92d	1971–1973	100	54	44	2	....	435	255	180	....	....
93d	1973–1975	100	56	42	2	....	435	242	192	1	....
94th	1975–1977	100	60	37	2	[5] 1	435	289	145	....	1
95th	1977–1979	100	61	38	1	....	435	292	143	....	....

[1] Democrats organized House with help of other parties.
[2] Democrats organized House, due to Republican deaths.
[3] Proclamation declaring Alaska a State issued Jan. 3, 1959.
[4] Proclamation declaring Hawaii a State issued Aug 21, 1959.
[5] New Hampshire election undecided.

THE EXECUTIVE

108. How many Presidents have had previous service in Congress?

Twenty-three. Of the 23, seven had served in the House only (James Madison, James K. Polk, Millard Fillmore, Abraham Lincoln, Rutherford B. Hayes, William McKinley, and Gerald Ford), six in the Senate only (James Monroe, John Quincy Adams, Martin Van Buren, Benjamin Harrison, Warren G. Harding, and Harry S. Truman), and 10 in both Houses (Andrew Jackson, William Henry Harrison, John Tyler, Franklin Pierce, James Buchanan, Andrew Johnson, James A. Garfield, John F. Kennedy, Lyndon B. Johnson, and Richard Nixon). In addition, George Washington, John Adams, Thomas Jefferson, James Madison, and James Monroe served in the Continental Congress.

109. What qualifications are prescribed for the President?

He must be a natural-born citizen, at least 35 years old, and for at least 14 years a resident of the United States. The question as to whether a child born abroad of American parents is "a natural-born citizen," in the sense of this clause, has been frequently debated. The answer depends upon whether the definition of "citizens of the United States" in section 1 of the 14th amendment is to be given an exclusive or an inclusive interpretation.

110. What is the wording of the oath taken by the President? Who administers it?

The form of oath for the President is prescribed by the Constitution as follows:

"I do solemnly swear (or affirm) that I will faithfully execute the office of President of the United States, and will, to the best of my ability, preserve, protect, and defend the Constitution of the United States."

Generally, the Chief Justice administers the oath, but this is merely custom. Any officer authorized to administer oaths could do it.

111. How is the President addressed?

Simply as "Mr. President." A letter sent to the Chief Executive is addressed "The President, The White House." One of the earliest congressional debates dealt with the title of the Chief Executive. A Senate committee recommended that the President be addressed, "His Highness, the President of the United States of America, and protector of their liberties." In the House, a debate on the subject was climaxed by James Madison's disclosure that the Constitution explicitly prescribed the Chief Magistrate's title as "President of the United States of America." When George Washington made his first inaugural address, the House made formal reply, addressing him simply as "The President of the United States." When the Senate's turn came to make a similar formal reply, the upper House reluctantly bowed to the precedent set by the lower House, but not without adopting a resolution declaring "that it would be proper to annex a respective title to the office" of President. "Thus it came about," writes Henry James Ford, "that the President of the United States is distinguished by having no title. A Governor is addressed as 'Your Excellency,' a judge as 'Your Honor,' but the Chief Magistrate of the Nation is simply 'Mr. President.' "

112. How is the date set for the commencement of a President's term?

By the Constitution. When the Constitution was ratified, the Congress was given the power to set the date for beginning the operations of the new government. Congress set the date of March 4, 1789, and although Washington did not take the oath of office until April 30, 1789, his term began as of March 4. Such remained the law until the 20th amendment became effective in 1937, and provided that the President's term should begin at noon on January 20, every four years.

113. What provision is made by the Constitution or by law for execution of the duties of President in event of the death, resignation, or disability of the Chief Executive, or his removal from office?

Under article II, section 1, the Vice President exercises the powers and duties of the President in such case. The 25th amendment, ratified by the required three-fourths of the States on February 10, 1967, provides: (1) that a Vice President who succeeds a President acquires all the powers of the office; (2) that when the Vice Presidency is vacant, it shall be filled by nomination by the President when confirmed by a majority vote of both Houses of Congress; (3) that when the President informs Congress he is unable to discharge his duties and until he informs Congress otherwise, the Vice President shall act as President; (4) a procedure by which Congress would settle disputes between a Vice President and a President as to the latter's ability to discharge the powers and duties of his office. A law of July 18, 1947, sets the line of succession after the Vice President through the Speaker of the House of Representatives, the President pro tempore of the Senate, and certain members of the Cabinet beginning with the Secretary of State.

Richard Nixon is the only President ever to resign; on August 9, 1974, under threat of impeachment and removal from office by the Congress (see also question 88 on impeachment and 136 on Vice Presidential resignations).

114. What would happen if the President-elect were to die before taking office?

This situation has never yet occurred. If the President-elect were to die before the Electoral College had voted (the second Wednesday in December), a new presidential candidate would be named by the party organization. If the President-elect were to die after the Electoral College had voted, the Vice President-elect would become President the following January 20.

115. Who would succeed to the Presidency if the President-elect and the Vice President-elect failed to qualify prior to Inauguration Day?

The Speaker of the House of Representatives. In the event he should be disqualified, the President pro tempore of the Senate and then in the following order: Secretary of State, Secretary of the Treasury, Secretary of Defense, Attorney General, Secretary of the Interior, Secretary of Agriculture, Secretary of Commerce, Secretary of Labor, Secretary of Health, Education, and Welfare, Secretary of Housing and Urban Development, Secretary of Transportation, and Secretary of Energy.

116. What is the salary attached to the Presidency?

The President's salary is $200,000 a year, subject to income tax the same as other citizens' salaries.

117. What allowances does the President receive?

The President lives officially in the White House, although curiously enough the law merely grants him the use of the furniture and other effects belonging to the United States and kept in the Executive Mansion.

The President receives $50,000 annually (taxable) for expenses of official duties. In addition, he may spend up to $40,000 annually (nontaxable) for travel expenses and official entertainment.

A President-elect who is not the incumbent President, is, upon request, provided with necessary facilities and equipment to prepare him for assumption of his duties as President including suitable office space appropriately equipped with furnishings and office supplies. He is also supplied with funds to compensate members of his office staff at rates determined by him but not to exceed a Civil Service level of GS–18. Also, any employee of any agency of any branch of the Government may be detailed to such staff, responsible only to the President-elect but with continuance of compensation and other benefits from his former position without interruption. Payments may also be provided for the following: procurement of services of experts or organizations as consultants (not to exceed $100 per diem per individual), travel allowances for persons employed by him intermittently with or without compensation, communications services, printing and binding expenses and postage.

118. Do former Presidents and their widows receive a pension?

Each former President is entitled to receive annually for the remainder of his life an amount equal to the salary of the head of an executive department (presently $66,000). He is entitled to $96,000 per year for office staff selected by him at rates of compensation set by him. A former President is also furnished with suitable office space and is granted free use of the mail.

The widow of a President is entitled to receive a pension of $20,000 per year if she waives the right to any annuity or pension under any other act of Congress and does not remarry before becoming 60 years of age.

Subject to the direction of the Secretary of the Treasury, the U.S. Secret Service is authorized to protect a former President and his 'wife during his lifetime, the widow of a President until her death or remarriage, and minor children of a former President until they reach the age of sixteen, unless such protection is declined.

119. What are the constitutional powers of the President?

Article II of the Constitution vests the "executive power" in the President. There is dispute among scholars as to whether the executive power consists solely of those powers enumerated for the President or whether it consists of those powers that are implied in Article II. Most authorities lean toward the latter interpretation.

The actual powers expressly granted to the President are few in number. He is Commander in Chief of the Army and Navy and of the state militias when called into the service of the United States. He may require the written opinion of his executive officers and is empowered to grant reprieves and pardons except in the case of impeachment. He has power, by and with the advice and consent of the Senate, to make treaties, provided that two-thirds of the Senators present concur. He also nominates, and by and with the advice and consent of the Senate, appoints Ambassadors, other public ministers and consuls, Justices of the Supreme Court, and other Federal officers whose appointments are established by law. Congress has by law vested the appointment of inferior officers in the President. The President has the power to fill all vacancies that occur during the recess of the Senate. Those commissions expire unless the Senate consents to them when it reconvenes. The Constitution also directs the President periodically to inform Congress on the state of the Union and to recommend legislation that he considers necessary and expedient. He may, on extraordinary occasions, convene both Houses of Congress, or either of them, and in case the two Houses disagree as to the time of adjournment he may adjourn them to such time as he shall think proper. The President shall also receive Ambassadors and other public ministers, take care that the laws are faithfully executed, and commission all officers of the United States. The President may veto acts of Congress. A two-thirds vote of those present and voting is required in both the House and the Senate to override his veto.

120. Has it always been customary for Presidents to appear before joint sessions of the House and Senate to deliver messages?

Presidents Washington and John Adams appeared before the two Houses in joint session to read their messages. Jefferson discontinued the practice in 1801, transmitting his message to the Capitol to be read by the clerks in both Houses. Jefferson's procedure was followed for a full century. On April 8, 1913, Wilson revived the practice of addressing the Congress in person. With the exception of Hoover the practice has been followed generally by subsequent Presidents.

121. What is meant by "executive privilege"?

The President invokes the right of "executive privilege" when he decides to withhold information from Congress. Denial may be based on the need for secrecy, which was one of the reasons offered by President Washington when he refused to give the House of Representatives certain papers on the Jay Treaty. Other Presidents have invoked the privilege on the ground that disclosure of information may violate the confidence and trust that has to exist between the President and his assistants. In 1974 the Supreme Court in *Nixon* v. *U.S.* recognized the President's right to "executive privilege," but at the same time restricted its application by ruling that the President may not withhold evidence needed in criminal proceedings by invoking that privilege.

122. What is an executive order?

Executive authorities often issue rules and regulations to implement legislation and set forth efficient procedures for internal administration. Sometimes these are in the form of an executive order by the President. In the event that an executive order exceeds the bounds of presidential authority, the Supreme Court may declare it invalid.

123. What is the Federal Register System?

The Federal Register System, established in 1935 by the Federal Register Act, is the means by which administrative rules and regulations issued by executive departments and agencies under authority of law are codified and made known to the public. It consists of the *Federal Register*, published daily Tuesday through Saturday except for the day following a legal holiday; the *Code of Federal Regulations*, an annually issued multi-volume cumulation of administrative regulations in force; and the annually published *United States Government Organization Manual*. The System is administered by the National Archives and Records Service of the General Services Administration.

124. What kinds of documents are published in the *Federal Register*?

There are four basic kinds of documents which must be published in the *Federal Register* before they are considered legally binding: (1) presidential proclamations and executive orders of general interest, and any other document the President submits or orders to be published; (2) every document issued under proper authority which prescribes a penalty or course of conduct; confers a right, privilege, authority, or immunity; or imposes an obligation, and which is relevant or applicable to the general public, members of a class of people, or persons of a locality; (3) documents or classes of documents required by act of Congress to be filed and published; and (4) other documents deemed by the Director of the Federal Register to be of sufficient interest. Although the *Federal Register* is unknown to many citizens, it constitutes a major means of regulating and governing in the United States.

125. What is an "executive agreement"?

It is an international agreement between the President and a foreign government in which the Senate's advice and consent is not required. Many of these agreements are based upon statutory support (such as reciprocal trade agreements) or are pursuant to a treaty provision. Others, however, result solely from Presidential initiative. Among the more important examples in this latter class are the Destroyers-Bases deal with Great Britain in 1940 and the Yalta and Potsdam Agreements in 1945.

126. What are the official duties of the Cabinet?

Cabinet members, as such, have no official duties, but are recognized as the President's regular advisers. They meet in the Cabinet room of the executive offices in the White House.

127. What are the Government positions held by members of the President's Cabinet?

Secretary of State, Secretary of the Treasury, Secretary of Defense, Attorney General, Secretary of the Interior, Secretary of Agriculture, Secretary of Commerce, Secretary of Labor, Secretary of Health, Education, and Welfare, Secretary of Housing and Urban Development, Secretary of Transportation, and Secretary of Energy. The Vice President and certain other officials of the executive branch have been invited by the President to participate in Cabinet meetings.

128. What salary does a Cabinet member receive?

Sixty-six thousand dollars annually.

129. May the Secretary of State or any other Cabinet officer appear on the floor of either House to answer questions?

No. There has been considerable agitation since 1919 for extending the privilege of the floor to Cabinet members for the purpose of asking questions, but numerous measures to this effect have failed to be enacted.

Cabinet members, however, do appear before committees of the two Houses to give testimony, and they may visit either House while in session.

130. How did the Postal Reorganization and Salary Adjustment Act of 1970 change the Post Office Department?

The United States Postal Service is now an independent agency within the executive branch. It operates under an 11-member board of governors, nine of whom are appointed by the President, with the concurrence of the Senate, for staggered, 9-year terms. Not more than five may be of the same political party. These nine then select from outside their ranks a Postmaster General, who is chairman of the board. He, together with the board, chooses a Deputy Postmaster General.

The President also appoints an 11-member advisory council for two-year terms. Four of the members represent the major mailers, four the postal workers, and three the general public.

Postal rates are to be set by a Postal Rate Commission, composed of five presidentially appointed members. This Commission sets rates subject only to unanimous veto by the Board of Governors or to judicial review.

The Postal Service is authorized to issue $10 billion in bonds to finance its operations. In addition, there will be an annual subsidy from Congress through 1984.

Salary increases for postal employees are to be determined by collective bargaining.

131. What are independent agencies and regulatory commissions?

The independent agencies, in general, comprise all federal executive agencies not included under the 12 executive departments or within the Executive Office of the President. Some of them, such as the Smithsonian Institution, are of long standing. Many others have been created in recent years, as the responsibilities of the Government have increased. A regulatory commission is an independent agency established by Congress to regulate some aspect of American economic life. Among these are the Securities and Exchange Commission, the Interstate Commerce Commission, and others. Such agencies are, of course, not independent of the U.S. Government. They are subject to the laws under which they operate as these laws are enacted by Congress and executed by the President.

132. Has a Vice President of the United States ever been elected by the Senate?

One—Richard M. Johnson of Kentucky. In the 1836 election, Johnson received 147 electoral votes; Granger, 77; Tyler, 47; and Smith, 23. Johnson's total equaled that of the combined votes for the other three, but he lacked a majority. The Constitution provides that in such instances the Senate must choose between the two highest candidates whenever any fails to obtain a majority of all electoral votes. The Senate elected Johnson.

133. How many Vice Presidents have succeeded to the Presidency by reason of a vacancy in that office?

Nine: Tyler, Fillmore, Andrew Johnson, Arthur, Theodore Roosevelt, Coolidge, Truman, Lyndon B. Johnson, and Ford.

134. Of these successions, how many were caused by the assassination of Presidents?

Four: Lincoln, McKinley, Garfield, and Kennedy were killed by assassins. Andrew Johnson served as President during all but 1 month of Lincoln's second term; Theodore Roosevelt served $3\frac{1}{2}$ years of McKinley's second term; Chester A. Arthur served about $3\frac{1}{2}$ years of Garfield's term; and Lyndon B. Johnson served about $1\frac{1}{4}$ years of Kennedy's term.

135. What salary and expenses does the President of the Senate (Vice President) receive annually?

Salary, $75,000 (taxable); expense allowance, $10,000 (taxable). This applies either to the Vice President of the United States, who is President of the Senate, or to the President pro tempore of the Senate in the event there is no Vice President.

The Vice President also receives allowances for clerk hire, stationery, and postage. Civil Service retirement benefits have been extended to the Vice President.

A Vice President-elect, who is not the incumbent President or Vice President, upon request is provided with the same necessary facilities, equipment, and allowances as a President-elect.

136. Has a Vice President ever resigned?

Two Vice Presidents have resigned. John C. Calhoun resigned on December 28, 1832, three months before the expiration of his term, to become Senator from South Carolina. Spiro Agnew resigned October 10, 1973 subsequent to pleading *nolo contendere* (no contest) to a charge of Federal income tax evasion. Pursuant to Mr. Agnew's resignation, President Nixon nominated Gerald R. Ford, the Minority Leader of the House, to fill the vice presidential vacancy. The Senate and House, in accordance with the provisions of the Twenty-fifth Amendment under which Mr. Ford had been nominated, approved the nomination and Mr. Ford was sworn in December 6, 1973. Less than a year later Mr. Ford became President subsequent to Richard Nixon's resignation. On August 20, 1974 he nominated Nelson Rockefeller to be Vice President, who was confirmed and sworn in December 10, 1974. Thus, in less than one year two occasions arose for using the provisions of the Twenty-fifth Amendment to fill a vacancy in the vice presidency.

THE JUDICIARY

137. Does the Constitution prescribe qualifications for Federal judges?

The Constitution does not state what qualifications are demanded of men for these offices, either as to age, citizenship, legal competence, or as to political viewpoint and background.

138. Who was the youngest Supreme Court Justice to serve on the Nation's highest tribunal?

The youngest was Joseph Story, who became a member of the Supreme Court at the age of 32 and served from 1811 to 1845. Only three other Justices have been named to the Court before their 40th birthdays: Justices James Iredell, Bushrod Washington, and William Johnson.

139. What is the Chief Justice's official title?

The first seven Chief Justices—Jay, Rutledge, Ellsworth, Marshall, Taney, Chase, and Waite—were referred to as "Chief Justice of the Supreme Court of the United States." The next eight—Fuller, White, Taft, Hughes, Stone, Vinson, Warren, and Burger—were designated as "Chief Justice of the United States."

140. What is the difference between opinions and decisions of the Supreme Court?

An opinion is the statement of the reasoning by which the Court fortifies a decision in a particular case. The decision is reached by secret vote of the Justices, and the Chief Justice then assigns a Justice the task of writing the opinion.

141. What is a Supreme Court quorum?

Currently, six Justices constitute a quorum.

142. What are the salaries of Supreme Court Justices?

The Chief Justice of the United States receives $75,000 annually and each Associate Justice $72,000 annually. The Constitution provides that the salaries of Federal judges shall not be reduced during their tenure of office.

143. Who determines the number of members constituting the Supreme Court?

Congress fixes the number of members and their salaries. By an Act of June 25, 1948, there are eight Associate Justices.

144. Does the Supreme Court review every case it receives?

The majority of cases are disposed of by the brief decision that the subject matter is either not proper or not of sufficient importance to warrant Court review. Each year only 250 to 300 cases of importance are decided on their merits; about half of these decisions are announced in full published opinions.

145. When does the Supreme Court meet?

The Supreme Court meets on the first Monday in October for a session which generally extends to mid-June. The sessions which begin at 10 a.m. and last until 2:30 are open to the public Monday through Thursday. On Friday, the Justices assemble for their private weekly conferences. It is then that the cases which have been presented to them are discussed and voted upon.

146. Are Supreme Court decisions announced during public sessions of the tribunal?

The Justices disclose their decisions after they have met in executive session to discuss their views and to vote. During these discussions, every Justice expresses his findings and conclusions fully. The meeting culminates with a vote conducted by the Chief Justice, who calls upon his associates in reverse order according to the dates of their commissions. In many instances the Justices individually arrive at their decisions after arguments in the case have been heard, but such decisions remain secret until after the executive session and the vote.

147. Has it always been customary for one Justice to deliver the majority opinion?

It has not always been the practice of the Court to have one Justice deliver the majority and another the minority opinion. Originally the Justices delivered their own opinions, *seriatim*, whether in agreement with the majority or the minority. Chief Justice Marshall introduced the timesaving procedure of delivering one opinion for the Court. This proved desirable as the Court's business increased.

148. What are the District Courts of the United States?

The District Courts are the trial courts with general Federal jurisdiction. Each state and the District of Columbia has at least one District Court; many states have two or three districts, and Texas and New York have four districts each. There are 94 of these courts, 89 in the 50 states and one each in the District of Columbia, the Canal Zone, Guam, Puerto Rico, and the Virgin Islands. A district may be divided into divisions and may have several places where the court hears cases. Cases from the District Courts are reviewed by the U.S. Courts of Appeals, except that injunction orders of special three-judge District Courts, certain decisions holding acts of Congress unconstitutional, and certain criminal decisions may be appealed directly to the Supreme Court.

149. What are the U.S. Courts of Appeals?

The Courts of Appeals are intermediate appellate courts, created by Act of March 3, 1891, to relieve the Supreme Court of considering all appeals in cases originally decided by the Federal trial courts. They are empowered to review all final decisions and certain interlocutory decisions of District Courts, except in those very few situations where the law provides for a direct review by the Supreme Court. They also are empowered to review and enforce orders of many Federal administrative bodies, such as the Securities and Exchange Commission and the National Labor Relations Board. The decisions of the Courts of Appeals are final except as they are subject to discretionary review or appeal in the Supreme Court.

150. What are the special courts of the United States?

In addition to the Supreme Court, the U.S. Courts of Appeals, and the U.S. District Courts, special courts have been created by Congress to deal with particular types of cases. Appeals from the decisions of the U.S. Court of Claims, the U.S. Court of Customs and Patent Appeals, and the U.S. Tax Court (except for certain kinds of decisions regarding excess profits) may ultimately be reviewed in the Supreme Court. An additional special court, the U.S. Court of Military Appeals is established as the final appellate tribunal in court-martial convictions. It is judicially independent although it operates as a part of the Department of Defense for administrative purposes.

CENSUS FIGURES BY STATE [1]

State	1970	1960	Change, 1960 to 1970	
			Number	Percent
United States	203, 184, 772	179, 323, 175	23, 861, 597	13. 3
Alabama	3, 444, 165	3, 266, 740	177, 425	5. 4
Alaska	302, 173	226, 167	76, 006	33. 6
Arizona	1, 772, 482	1, 302, 161	470, 321	36. 1
Arkansas	1, 923, 295	1, 786, 272	137, 023	7. 7
California	19, 953, 134	15, 717, 204	4, 235, 930	27. 0
Colorado	2, 207, 259	1, 753, 947	453, 312	25. 8
Connecticut	3, 032, 217	2, 535, 234	496, 983	19. 6
Delaware	548, 104	446, 292	101, 812	22. 8
District of Columbia	756, 510	763, 956	−7, 446	−1. 0
Florida	6, 789, 443	4, 951, 550	1, 837, 883	37. 1
Georgia	4, 589, 575	3, 943, 116	646, 459	16. 4
Hawaii	769, 913	632, 772	137, 141	21. 7
Idaho	713, 008	667, 191	45, 817	6. 9
Illinois	11, 113, 976	10, 081, 158	1, 032, 818	10. 2
Indiana	5, 193, 669	4, 662, 498	531, 171	11. 4
Iowa	2, 825, 041	2, 757, 537	67, 504	2. 4
Kansas	2, 249, 071	2, 178, 611	70, 460	3. 2
Kentucky	3, 219, 311	3, 038, 156	181, 155	6. 0
Louisiana	3, 643, 180	3, 257, 022	386, 158	11. 9
Maine	993, 663	969, 265	24, 398	2. 5
Maryland	3, 922, 399	3, 100, 689	821, 710	26. 5
Massachusetts	5, 689, 170	5, 148, 578	540, 592	10. 5
Michigan	8, 875, 083	7, 823, 194	1, 051, 889	13. 4
Minnesota	3, 805, 069	3, 413, 865	391, 205	11. 5
Mississippi	2, 261, 912	2, 178, 141	38, 771	1. 8
Missouri	4, 677, 399	4, 319, 813	357, 568	8. 3
Montana	694, 409	674, 767	19, 642	2. 9
Nebraska	1, 483, 791	1, 411, 330	72, 461	5. 1
Nevada	488, 738	285, 278	203, 460	71. 3
New Hampshire	737, 681	606, 921	130, 760	21. 5
New Jersey	7, 168, 164	6, 066, 782	1, 101, 382	18. 2
New Mexico	1, 016, 000	951, 023	64, 977	6. 8
New York	18, 190, 740	16, 782, 304	1, 408, 436	8. 4
North Carolina	5, 082, 059	4, 556, 155	525, 904	11. 5
North Dakota	617, 761	632, 446	−14, 685	−2. 3
Ohio	10, 652, 017	9, 706, 397	945, 620	9. 7
Oklahoma	2, 559, 253	2, 328, 284	230, 969	9. 9
Oregon	2, 091, 385	1, 768, 687	322, 698	18. 2
Pennsylvania	11, 793, 909	11, 319, 366	474, 543	4. 2
Rhode Island	949, 723	859, 488	90, 235	10. 5
South Carolina	2, 590, 516	2, 382, 594	207, 922	8. 7
South Dakota	666, 257	680, 514	−14, 257	−2. 1
Tennessee	3, 924, 164	3, 567, 089	357, 075	10. 0
Texas	11, 196, 730	9, 579, 677	1, 617, 053	16. 9
Utah	1, 059, 273	890, 627	168, 646	18. 9
Vermont	444, 732	389, 881	54, 851	14. 1
Virginia	4, 648, 494	3, 966, 949	681, 545	17. 2
Washington	3, 409, 169	2, 853, 214	555, 955	19. 5
West Virginia	1, 744, 237	1, 860, 421	−116, 184	−6. 2
Wisconsin	4, 417, 933	3, 951, 777	466, 156	11. 8
Wyoming	332, 416	330, 066	2, 350	. 7

[1] Resident population only; does not include those temporarily residing overseas.

Source: Bureau of the Census.

GOVERNMENT HEADS AND CONGRESSIONAL OFFICIALS

President: Jimmy Carter
Vice President: Walter F. Mondale

THE CABINET
Secretary of State: Cyrus R. Vance
Secretary of the Treasury: W. Michael Blumenthal
Secretary of Defense: Harold Brown
Attorney General: Griffin B. Bell
Secretary of the Interior: Cecil D. Andrus
Secretary of Agriculture: Bob S. Bergland
Secretary of Commerce: Juanita M. Kreps
Secretary of Labor: F. Ray Marshall
Secretary of Health, Education, and Welfare: Joseph A. Califano, Jr.
Secretary of Housing and Urban Development: Patricia Roberts Harris
Secretary of Transportation: Brockman Adams
Secretary of Energy: James R. Schlesinger

SENATE
President of the Senate: Walter F. Mondale
President pro tempore of the Senate: James O. Eastland
Majority leader: Robert C. Byrd
Majority whip: Alan Cranston
Minority floor leader: Howard H. Baker, Jr.
Assistant minority leader: Ted Stevens

HOUSE OF REPRESENTATIVES
Speaker: Thomas P. O'Neill, Jr.
Majority leader: James C. Wright, Jr.
Majority whip: John Brademas
Chief deputy majority whip: Dan Rostenkowski (Illinois)
Deputy majority whips: Bill Alexander (Arkansas), George E. Danielson (California), Benjamin S. Rosenthal (New York)
Minority leader: John J. Rhodes
Minority whip: Robert H. Michel

STANDING COMMITTEES OF THE SENATE AND CHAIRMEN

Agriculture, Nutrition, and Forestry: Herman E. Talmadge
Appropriations: Warren G. Magnuson
Armed Services: John C. Stennis
Banking, Housing, and Urban Affairs: William Proxmire
Budget: Edmund S. Muskie
Commerce, Science, and Transportation: Howard W. Cannon
Energy and Natural Resources: Henry M. Jackson
Environment and Public Works: Jennings Randolph

Finance: Russell B. Long
Foreign Relations: John Sparkman
Governmental Affairs: Abraham A. Ribicoff
Human Resources: Harrison A. Williams, Jr.
Judiciary: James O. Eastland
Rules and Administration: Claiborne Pell
Veterans' Affairs: Alan Cranston

STANDING COMMITTEES OF THE HOUSE OF REPRESENTATIVES AND CHAIRMEN

Agriculture: Thomas S. Foley
Appropriations: George H. Mahon
Armed Services: Melvin Price
Banking, Finance and Urban Affairs: Henry S. Reuss
Budget: Robert N. Giaimo
District of Columbia: Charles C. Diggs, Jr.
Education and Labor: Carl D. Perkins
Government Operations: Jack Brooks
House Administration: Frank Thompson, Jr.
Interior and Insular Affairs: Morris K. Udall
International Relations: Clement J. Zablocki
Interstate and Foreign Commerce: Harley O. Staggers
Judiciary: Peter W. Rodino, Jr.
Merchant Marine and Fisheries: John M. Murphy
Post Office and Civil Service: Robert N. C. Nix
Public Works and Transportation: Harold T. Johnson
Rules: James J. Delaney
Science and Technology: Olin E. Teague
Small Business: Neal Smith
Standards of Official Conduct: John J. Flynt, Jr.
Veterans' Affairs: Ray Roberts
Ways and Means: Al Ullman

SENATE SELECT AND SPECIAL COMMITTEES AND CHAIRMEN

Select Committee on Ethics: Adlai E. Stevenson
Select Committee on Indian Affairs: James Abourezk
Select Committee on Intelligence: Birch Bayh
Select Committee on Small Business: Gaylord Nelson
Special Committee on Aging: Frank Church

HOUSE AD HOC AND SELECT COMMITTEES AND CHAIRMEN

Ad Hoc Select Committee on Outer Continental Shelf: John M. Murphy
Permanent Select Committee on Intelligence: Edward P. Boland
Select Committee on Aging: Claude Pepper
Select Committee on Assassinations: Louis Stokes
Select Committee on Congressional Operations: Jack Brooks
Select Committee on Ethics: Richardson Preyer
Select Committee on Narcotics Abuse and Control: Lester L. Wolff
Select Committee on Population: James H. Scheuer

HOUSE AND SENATE JOINT COMMITTEES AND CHAIRMEN

Economic: Richard Bolling
Library: Lucien N. Nedzi
Printing: Claiborne Pell
Taxation: Russell B. Long

JUSTICES OF THE SUPREME COURT

Warren E. Burger, *Chief Justice*
William J. Brennan, Jr., *Associate Justice*
Potter Stewart, *Associate Justice*
Byron R. White, *Associate Justice*
Thurgood Marshall, *Associate Justice*
Harry A. Blackmun, *Associate Justice*
Lewis F. Powell, *Associate Justice*
William H. Rehnquist, *Associate Justice*
John Paul Stevens, *Associate Justice*

INDEX

[Citations refer to question numbers except where noted]

Act: difference between bill and act, 77.

Amendment, to the Constitution: "lame duck," 13; number repealed, 11; procedure, 10; time permitted for ratification, 12.

Apportionment, 38–41.

Articles of Confederation, 3.

Attorney General, 127.

Bills: appropriations, 90; "dead," 86; deficiency, 91; difference between bill and act, 77; engrossed and enrolled, 74; first reading, 65; introduction by Member, 64; public, 76; rider, 92; sent to General Services Administration, 87; stages in House, 63; tax, 89; total number introduced since March 4, 1789, 79; veto, 80–85.

Bill of Rights: explanation of, 8; rights enumerated, 9.

Cabinet, 126–129.

Campaign financing and contributions, 18.

Census, figures by States comparing 1960 and 1970 population, p. 38.

Commissioner to Congress from Puerto Rico: committee assignments, distinguished from Congressman, pay, voting rights, 23, 24.

Committees: Committee of the Whole, 68; conference, 107; hearings, 102–103; House Rules Committee, 67; joint, 106; origins of, 95; select, 105; seniority rule, 100; services available to, 31; standing, 96–100; list of chairmen, pages 39–41.

Congress (also see House of Representatives; Representatives; Senate; Senator): adjournment and convening by President, 57; blacks in, 28; constitutional status, 19–20; galleries, 27; majority and minority leaders, 51–52; meeting time, 58; party conferences and caucuses, 54; political divisions, House and Senate, 1855–1979, page 28; rules and procedure, 50; services available to Members for legislative duties, 31, 54; session defined, length, 21; special sessions, 57; visitors, 27; "whips", duties of, 53; women in, 29.

Congressional Budget Office, 31.

Congressional districts: how determined, 39–40; equality of, 41.

Congressional Research Service: services to Members of Congress, 31.

Congressman. (Also see Congress; House of Representatives; Representatives; Senate; Senators.) Defined, 22; List of Members of Congress by State, pages IX–XIX.

Consent, unanimous, 61.

Constitution: as supreme law of land, 6; Bill of Rights, 8–9; how amended, procedure, 10; "lame duck" amendment, 13; number of amendments repealed, 11; preamble, 1; provision for electors, 14; provisions for "separation of powers" in the Federal Government, 7; six basic principles of, 5; time permitted for ratification of amendment, 15.

Courts of Appeals, U.S., 149.

Delegate to Congress: distinguished from a Congressman, pay, voting rights, 23–24; number in House, 23.

Democracy: and its American sources, 1–5.

Deputy President pro tempore, 24, 47.

Discharge petition: purpose and procedure, 104.

District Courts, U.S., 148.

Election Day, 16.

Elections (also see Electoral College; Presidents): regulation of, 17–18.

Electoral College, 14–15.

Executive Agreement, 121.

42

○

www.ingramcontent.com/pod-product-compliance
Lightning Source LLC
Chambersburg PA
CBHW022131280326
41933CB00007B/646